THE EASY BROADWAY FAKE BOOK

Melody, Lyrics and Simplified Chords

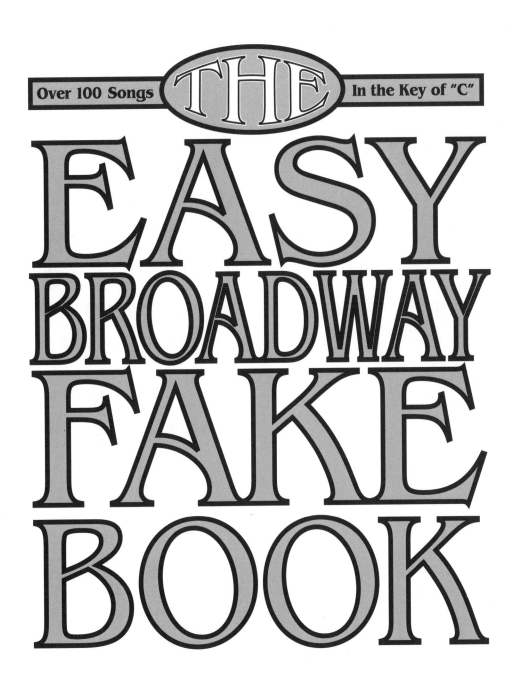

Over 100 Songs — **THE** — In the Key of "C"

EASY BROADWAY FAKE BOOK

ISBN 978-0-634-04126-6

HAL•LEONARD® CORPORATION

7777 W. BLUEMOUND RD. P.O. BOX 13819 MILWAUKEE, WI 53213

Visit Hal Leonard Online at
www.halleonard.com

THE EASY BROADWAY FAKE BOOK

CONTENTS

INTRODUCTION

What Is a Fake Book?

A fake book has one-line music notation consisting of melody, lyrics and chord symbols. This lead sheet format is a "musical shorthand" which is an invaluable resource for all musicians—hobbyists to professionals.

Here's how *The Easy Broadway Fake Book* differs from most standard fake books:

- All songs are in the key of C.

- Many of the melodies have been simplified.

- Only five basic chord types are used—major, minor, seventh, diminished and augmented.

- The music notation is larger for ease of reading.

In the event that you haven't used chord symbols to create accompaniment, or your experience is limited, a chord speller chart is included at the back of the book to help you get started.

Have fun!

AIN'T MISBEHAVIN'
from AIN'T MISBEHAVIN'

Words by ANDY RAZAF
Music by THOMAS "FATS" WALLER and HARRY BROOKS

ALL I ASK OF YOU
from THE PHANTOM OF THE OPERA

Music by ANDREW LLOYD WEBBER
Lyrics by CHARLES HART
Additional Lyrics by RICHARD STILGOE

Raoul:

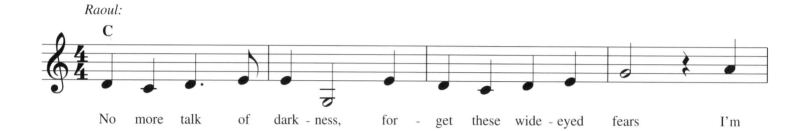

No more talk of dark - ness, for - get these wide - eyed fears I'm

here, noth - ing can harm you, my words will warm and calm you.

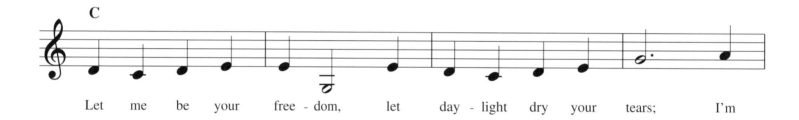

Let me be your free - dom, let day - light dry your tears; I'm

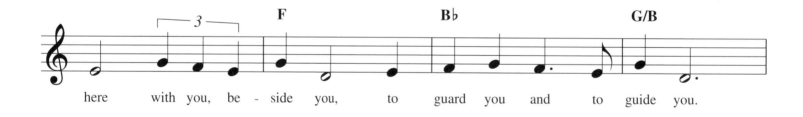

here with you, be - side you, to guard you and to guide you.

Christine:

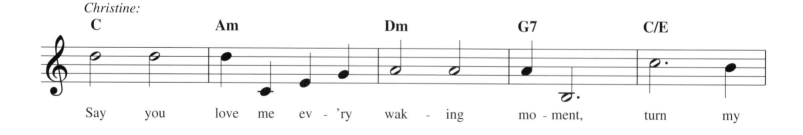

Say you love me ev - 'ry wak - ing mo - ment, turn my

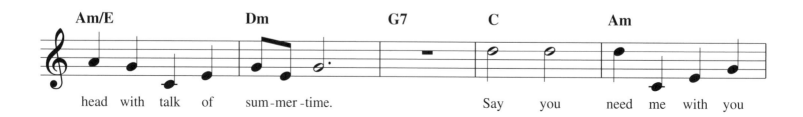

head with talk of sum - mer - time. Say you need me with you

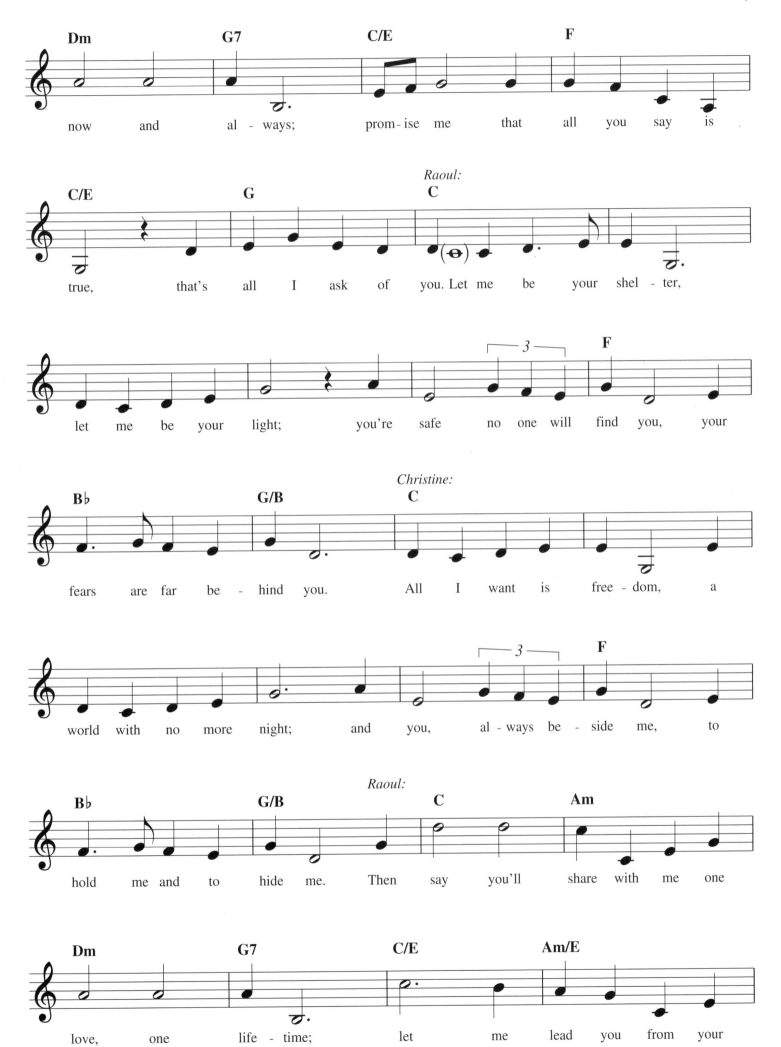

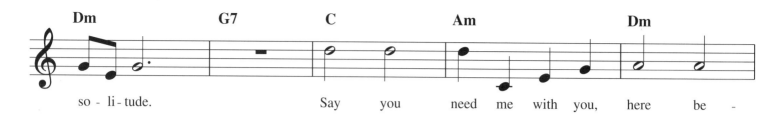

Dm — G7 — C — Am — Dm

so - li - tude. Say you need me with you, here be -

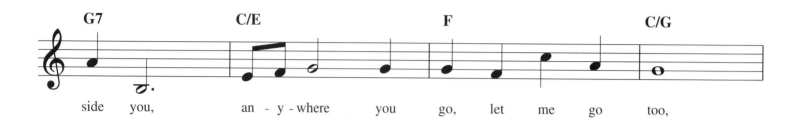

G7 — C/E — F — C/G

side you, an - y - where you go, let me go too,

Christine:

Dm/G — G7 — Am

Chris - tine, that's all I ask of you. Say you'll share with me one

Dm — G7 — C/E — Am/E

love, one life - time; say the word and I will

Together:

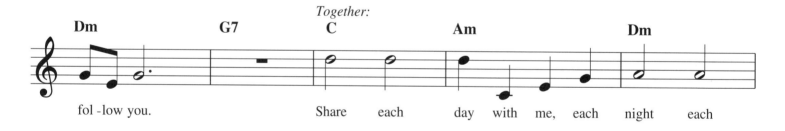

Dm — G7 — C — Am — Dm

fol - low you. Share each day with me, each night each

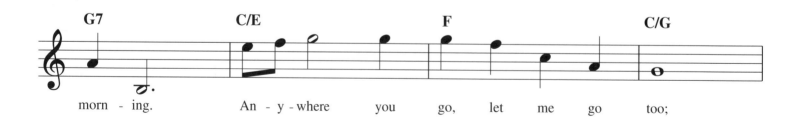

G7 — C/E — F — C/G

morn - ing. An - y - where you go, let me go too;

Dm/G — G7/B — C

love me, that's all I ask of you. _____

AS LONG AS HE NEEDS ME

from the Columbia Pictures - Romulus Motion Picture Production of Lionel Bart's OLIVER!

Words and Music by
LIONEL BART

ANOTHER OP'NIN', ANOTHER SHOW

from KISS ME, KATE

Words and Music by
COLE PORTER

An - oth - er op' - nin', an - oth - er show __
oth - er job _____ that you hope, at last, __

__ in Phil - ly, Bos - ton or Balt - i - mo'e, __
__ will make your fu - ture or for - get your past, __

__ a chance for stage - folks to say "Hel - lo" __
__ an - oth - er pain _____ where the ul - cers grow, __

an - oth - er op' - nin' of an - oth - er

show. An - show! Four weeks, _____ you re -

hearse and re - hearse, _____ three weeks, __

ANY DREAM WILL DO
from JOSEPH AND THE AMAZING TECHNICOLOR® DREAMCOAT

Music by ANDREW LLOYD WEBBER
Lyrics by TIM RICE

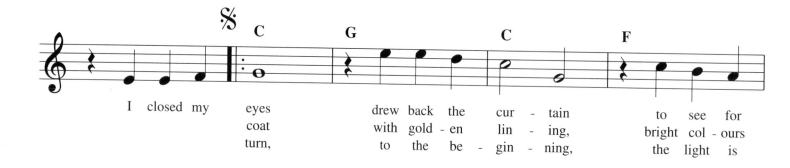

I closed my eyes
coat with gold-en lin-ing,
turn, to the be-gin-ning, the light is

drew back the cur-tain to see for
bright col-ours

cer-tain what I thought I knew. Far, far a-
shin-ing won-der-ful and new. And in the
dim-ming and the dream is too, the world and

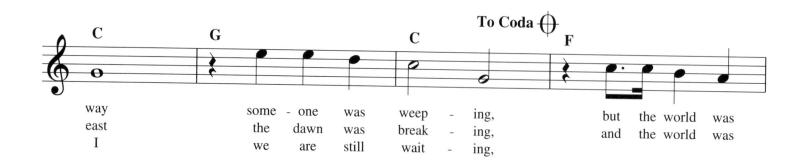

way some-one was weep-ing, but the world was
east the dawn was break-ing, and the world was
I we are still wait-ing,

sleep-ing, an-y dream will do. I wore my
wak-ing, an-y dream will

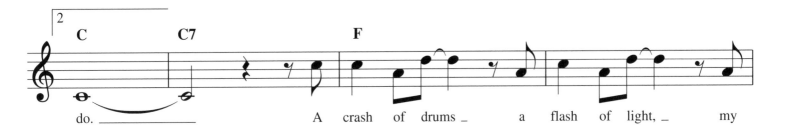

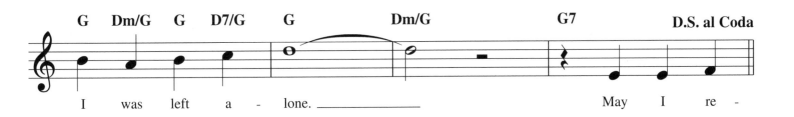

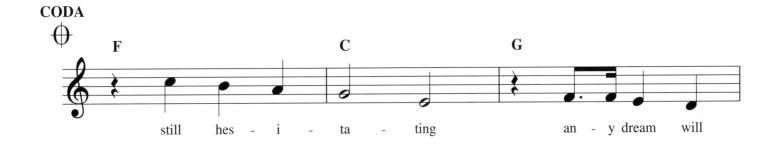

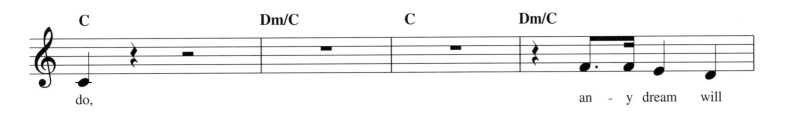

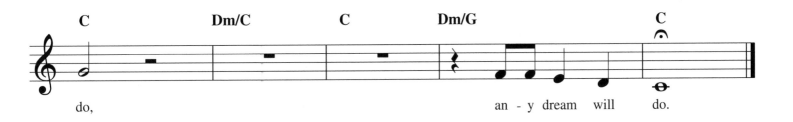

BALI HA'I

from SOUTH PACIFIC

Lyrics by OSCAR HAMMERSTEIN II
Music by RICHARD RODGERS

Ba - li Ha'i may call you an - y night, an - y

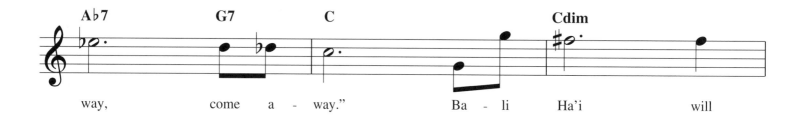

day. In your heart _____ you'll hear it call you: "Come a -

way, come a - way." Ba - li Ha'i will

whis - per on the wind of the sea: "Here am

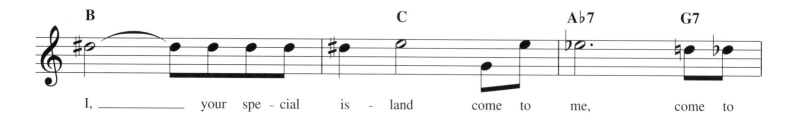

I, _____ your spe - cial is - land come to me, come to

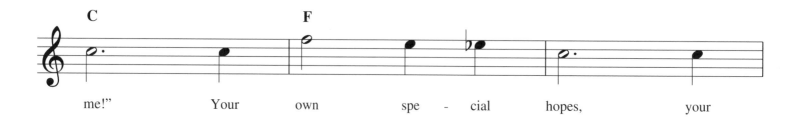

me!" Your own spe - cial hopes, your

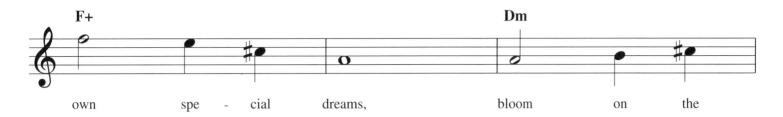

own   spe - cial   dreams,   bloom   on   the

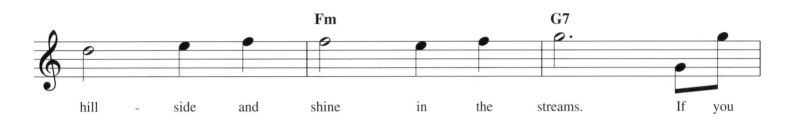

hill - side   and   shine   in   the   streams.   If   you

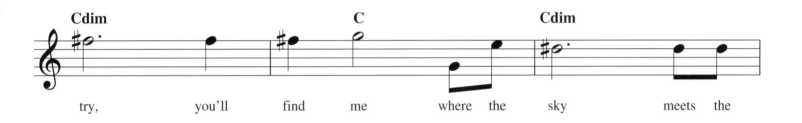

try,   you'll   find   me   where   the   sky   meets   the

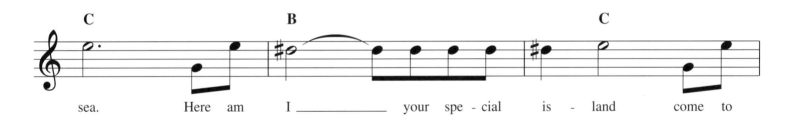

sea.   Here   am   I _____ your spe - cial   is - land   come   to

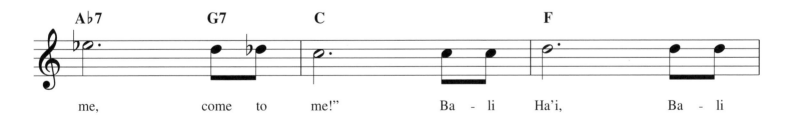

me,   come   to   me!"   Ba - li   Ha'i,   Ba - li

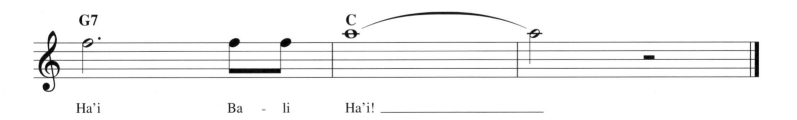

Ha'i   Ba - li   Ha'i! _____

BE KIND TO YOUR PARENTS

from FANNY

Words and Music by
HAROLD ROME

par - ents once were chil - dren long a - go. In -

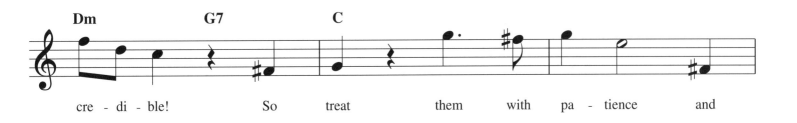

cre - di - ble! So treat them with pa - tience and

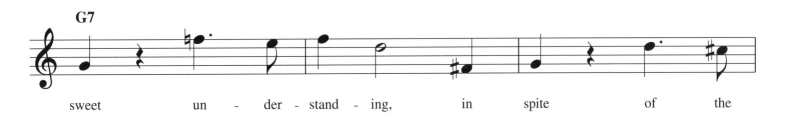

sweet un - der - stand - ing, in spite of the

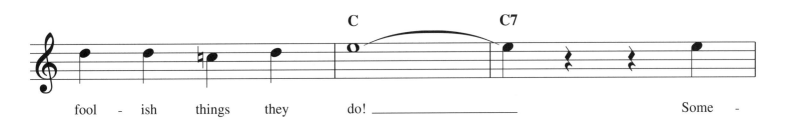

fool - ish things they do! _____ Some -

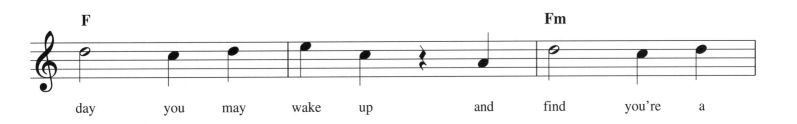

day you may wake up and find you're a

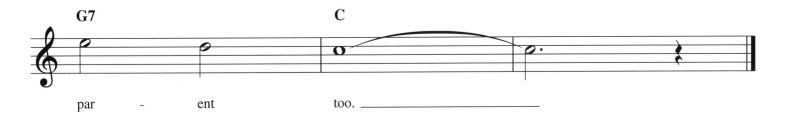

par - ent too. _____

BEAUTY AND THE BEAST
from Walt Disney's BEAUTY AND THE BEAST: THE BROADWAY MUSICAL

Lyrics by HOWARD ASHMAN
Music by ALAN MENKEN

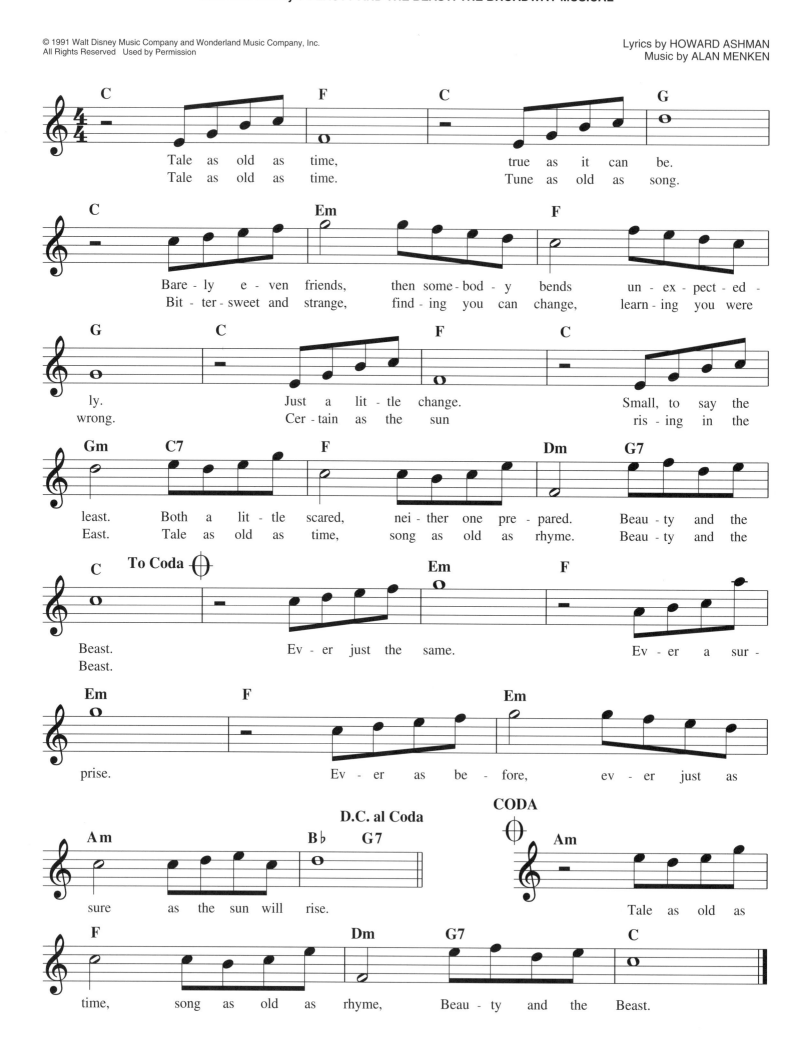

BROTHERHOOD OF MAN

from HOW TO SUCCEED IN BUSINESS WITHOUT REALLY TRYING

By FRANK LOESSER

BEWITCHED
from PAL JOEY

Words by LORENZ HART
Music by RICHARD RODGERS

I'm wild a - gain, be - guiled a - gain, a
Could - n't sleep and would - n't sleep when

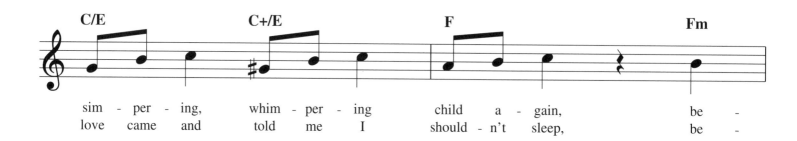

sim - per - ing, whim - per - ing child a - gain, be -
love came and told me I should - n't sleep, be -

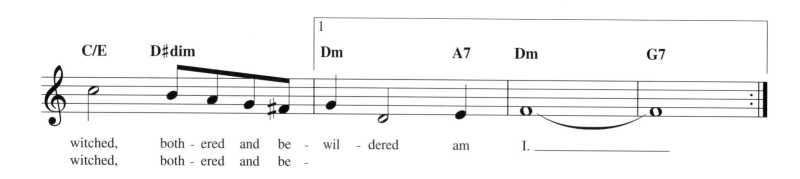

witched, both - ered and be - wil - dered am I.
witched, both - ered and be -

wil - dered am I. Lost my heart, but what

of it. He is cold, I a - gree.

He can laugh, but I love it, _____ al - though the laugh's on

me. I'll sing to him, each spring to him, and

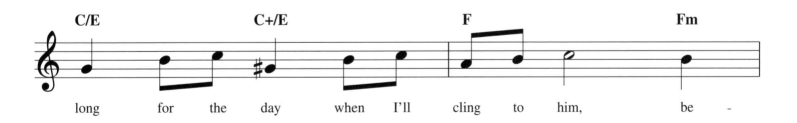

long for the day when I'll cling to him, be -

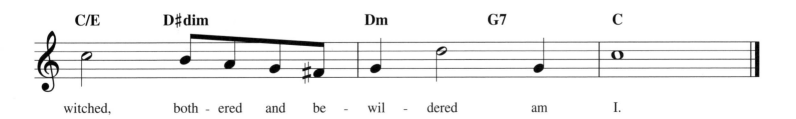

witched, both - ered and be - wil - dered am I.

BLUE SKIES
from BETSY

Words and Music by
IRVING BERLIN

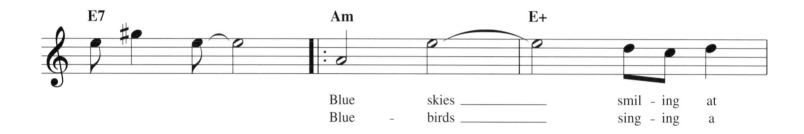

Blue   skies _____   smil - ing   at
Blue   -   birds _____   sing - ing   a

me. _____   Noth - ing   but   blue   skies _____
song; _____   noth - ing   but   blue   -   birds _____

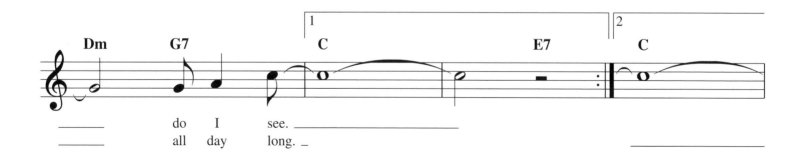

_____   do I   see. _____
_____   all day   long. _

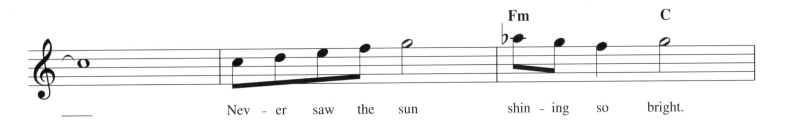

Nev - er saw the sun shin - ing so bright.

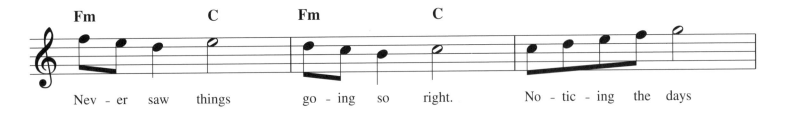

Nev - er saw things go - ing so right. No - tic - ing the days

hur - ry - ing by; when you're in love, my how they fly.

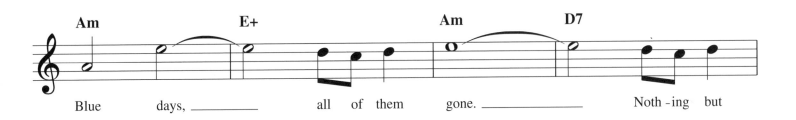

Blue days, _____ all of them gone. _____ Noth - ing but

blue skies _____ from now on. _____

BRING HIM HOME
from LES MISÉRABLES

Music by CLAUDE-MICHEL SCHÖNBERG
Lyrics by HERBERT KRETZMER and ALAIN BOUBLIL

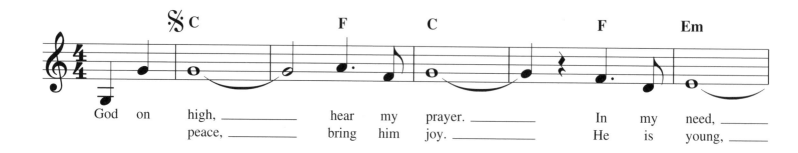

God on high, _____ hear my prayer. _____ In my need, _____
peace, _____ bring him joy. _____ He is young, _____

_____ you have al-ways been there. _____ He is young, _____
_____ he is on-ly a boy. _____ You can take, _____

_____ he's a-fraid. Let him rest, _____ heav-en blessed.
_____ you can give. Let him be, _____ let him live.

Bring him home, _____ bring him home, _____ bring him home.
If I die, _____ let me die, _____ let him

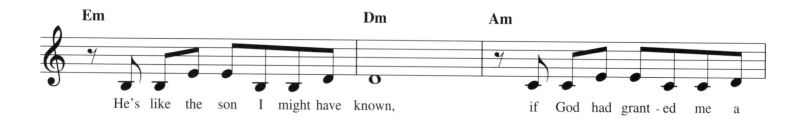

He's like the son I might have known, if God had grant-ed me a

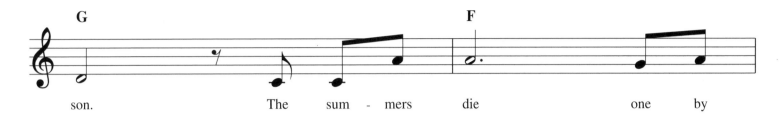

son. The sum - mers die one by

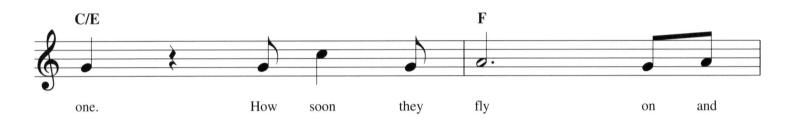

one. How soon they fly on and

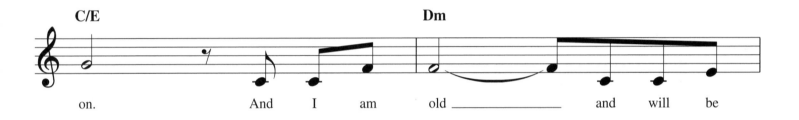

on. And I am old _____ and will be

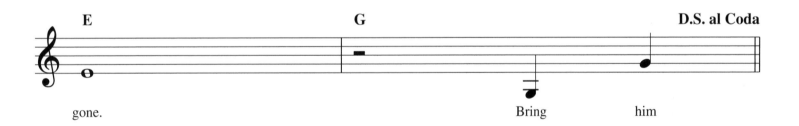

gone. Bring him

CODA

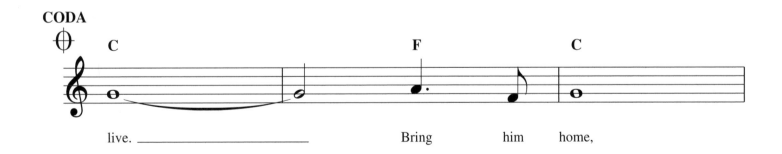

live. _____ Bring him home,

bring him home, _____ bring him home.

BRUSH UP YOUR SHAKESPEARE

from KISS ME, KATE

Words and Music by
COLE PORTER

27

CABARET
from the Musical CABARET

Words by FRED EBB
Music by JOHN KANDER

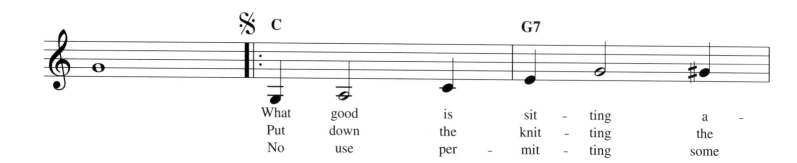

What   good   is   sit - ting   a -
Put   down   the   knit - ting   the
No   use   per - mit - ting   some

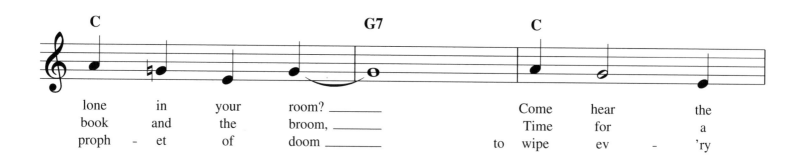

lone   in   your   room? _____   Come   hear   the
book   and   the   broom, _____   Time   for   a
proph - et   of   doom _____   to wipe   ev - 'ry

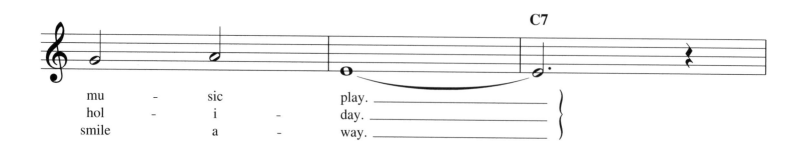

mu - sic   play. _____
hol - i - day. _____
smile   a - way. _____

To Coda ⊕

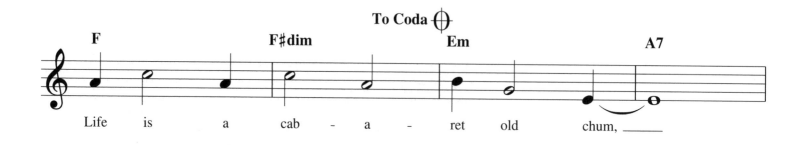

Life   is   a   cab - a - ret old   chum, _____

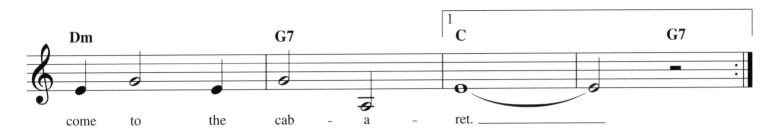

come to the cab - a - ret. _____

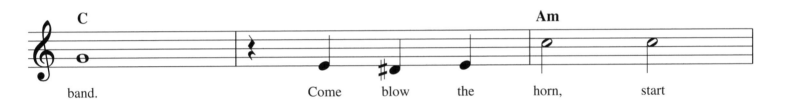

ret. Come taste the wine. Come hear the

band. Come blow the horn, start

cel - e - brat - ing, right this way, your ta - ble's wait - ing.

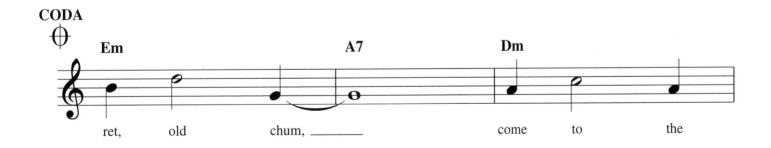

ret, old chum, _____ come to the

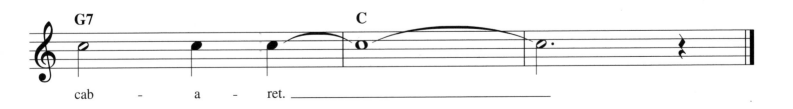

cab - a - ret. _____

CAMELOT
from CAMELOT

Words by ALAN JAY LERNER
Music by FREDERICK LOEWE

CAN YOU FEEL THE LOVE TONIGHT
Disney Presents THE LION KING: THE BROADWAY MUSICAL

Music by ELTON JOHN
Lyrics by TIM RICE

COMEDY TONIGHT
from A FUNNY THING HAPPENED ON THE WAY TO THE FORUM

Words and Music by
STEPHEN SONDHEIM

CLOSE EVERY DOOR

from JOSEPH AND THE AMAZING TECHNICOLOR® DREAMCOAT

Music by ANDREW LLOYD WEBBER
Lyrics by TIM RICE

CONSIDER YOURSELF

from the Columbia Pictures - Romulus Motion Picture Production of Lionel Bart's OLIVER!

Words and Music by
LIONEL BART

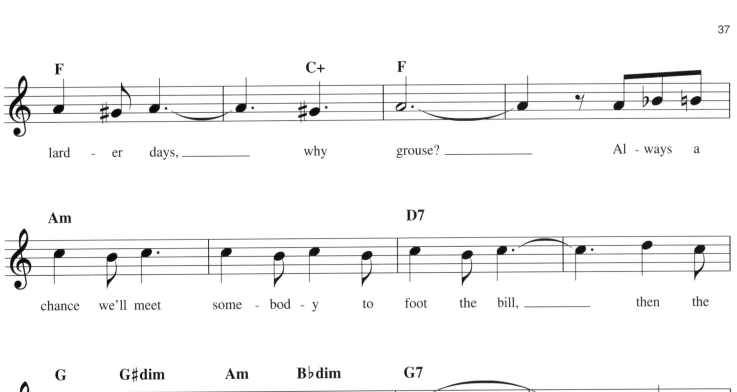

lard - er days, _____ why grouse? _____ Al - ways a

chance we'll meet some - bod - y to foot the bill, _____ then the

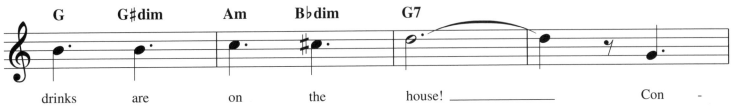

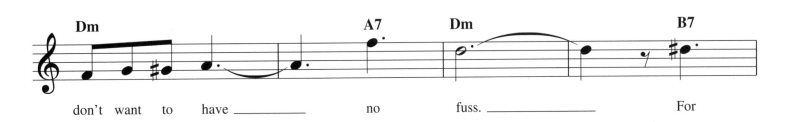

drinks are on the house! _____ Con -

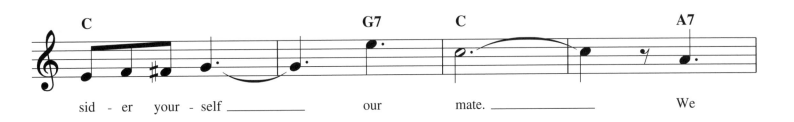

sid - er your - self _____ our mate. _____ We

don't want to have _____ no fuss. _____ For

af - ter some con - sid - er - a - tion, we can state: Con -

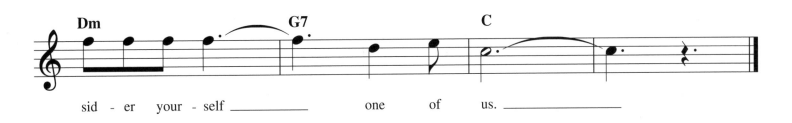

sid - er your - self _____ one of us. _____

EDELWEISS
from THE SOUND OF MUSIC

Lyrics by OSCAR HAMMERSTEIN II
Music by RICHARD RODGERS

GOODNIGHT, MY SOMEONE
from Meredith Willson's THE MUSIC MAN

By MEREDITH WILLSON

EVERYTHING'S COMING UP ROSES

from GYPSY

Words by STEPHEN SONDHEIM
Music by JULE STYNE

FALLING IN LOVE WITH LOVE
from THE BOYS FROM SYRACUSE

Words by LORENZ HART
Music by RICHARD RODGERS

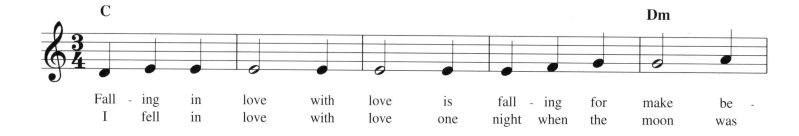

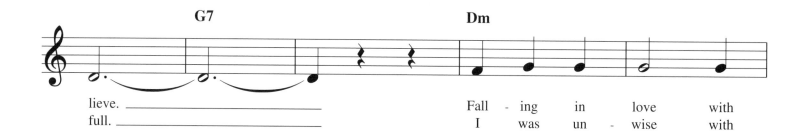

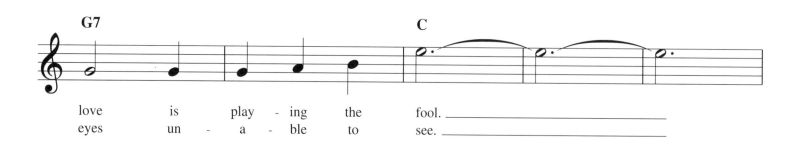

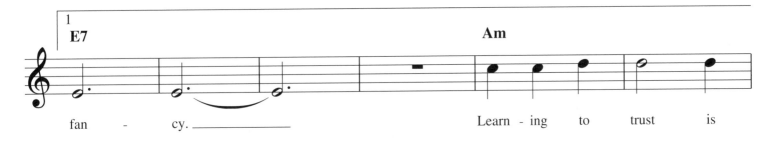

fan - cy. _____ Learn - ing to trust is

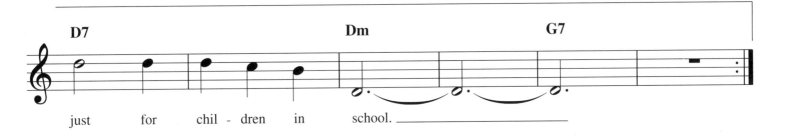

just for chil - dren in school. _____

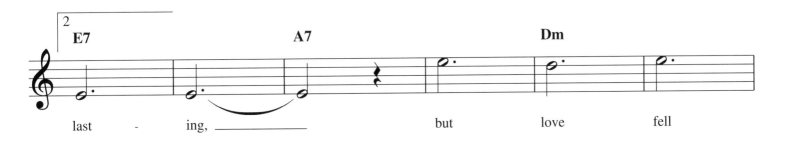

last - ing, _____ but love fell

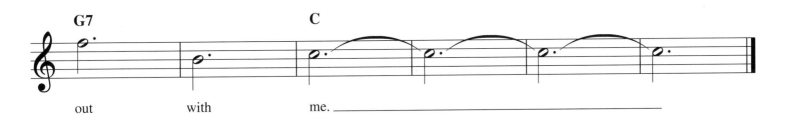

out with me. _____

GET ME TO THE CHURCH ON TIME

from MY FAIR LADY

Words by ALAN JAY LERNER
Music by FREDERICK LOEWE

I'm get - tin' mar - ried in the morn - ing. _____
I got - ta be there in the morn - ing. _____

Ding! Dong! The bells are gon - na chime. _____
Spruced up and look - ing in my prime. _____

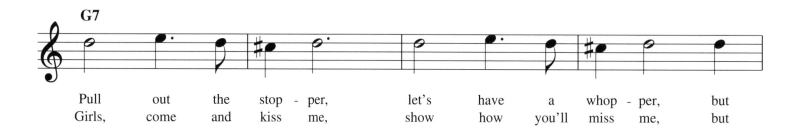

Pull out the stop - per, let's have a whop - per, but
Girls, come and kiss me, show how you'll miss me, but

get me to the church on time. _____
get me to the church on

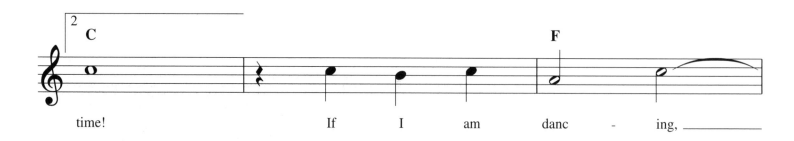

time! If I am danc - ing, _____

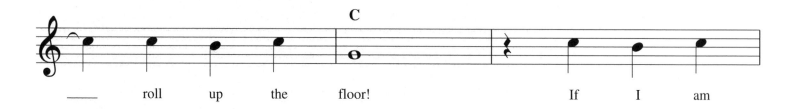

____ roll up the floor! If I am

whist - ling, whewt me out the door. For

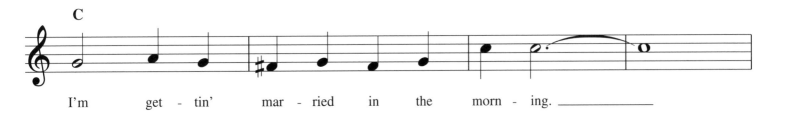

I'm get - tin' mar - ried in the morn - ing. _____

Ding! Dong! The bells are gon - na chime. _____

Kick up a rum - pus, but don't lose the com - pass; and

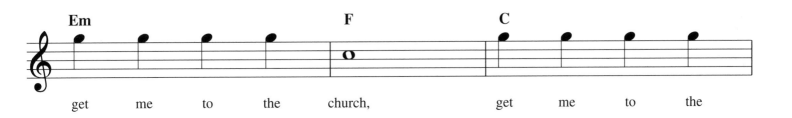

get me to the church, get me to the

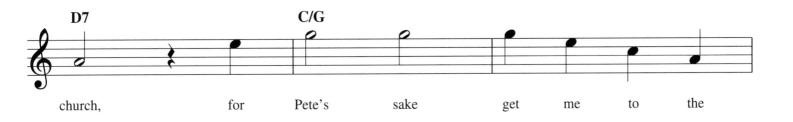

church, for Pete's sake get me to the

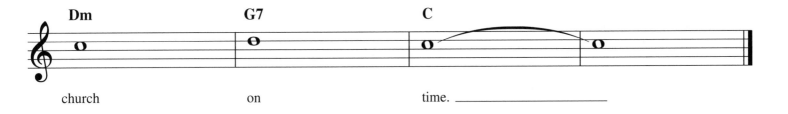

church on time. _____

GETTING TO KNOW YOU
from THE KING AND I

Lyrics by OSCAR HAMMERSTEIN II
Music by RICHARD RODGERS

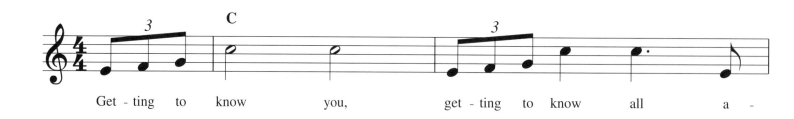

Get - ting to know you, get - ting to know all a -

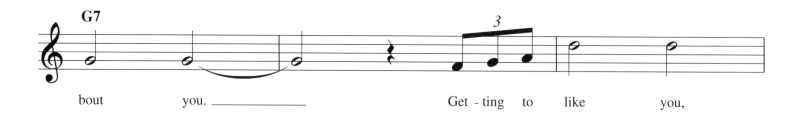

bout you. _____ Get - ting to like you,

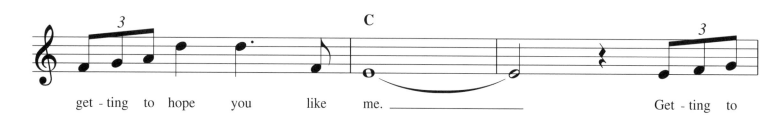

get - ting to hope you like me. _____ Get - ting to

know you, put - ting it my way but nice - ly, _____

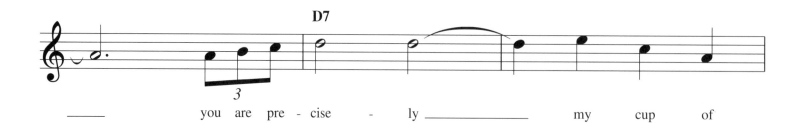

_____ you are pre - cise - ly _____ my cup of

tea. _____ Get - ting to know you,

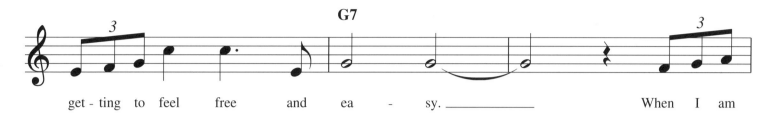

get - ting to feel free and ea - sy. _____ When I am

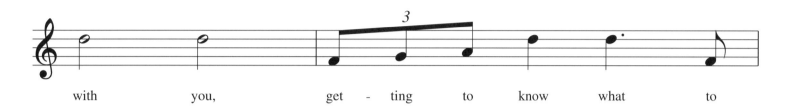

with you, get - ting to know what to

say. _____ Have - n't you no - ticed,

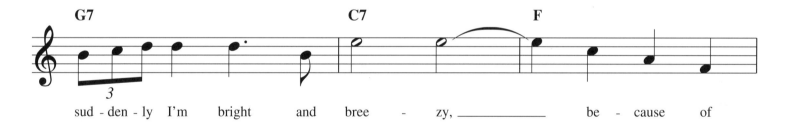

sud - den - ly I'm bright and bree - zy, _____ be - cause of

all the beau - ti - ful and new things I'm

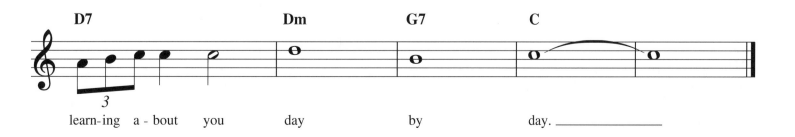

learn-ing a - bout you day by day. _____

GUYS AND DOLLS
from GUYS AND DOLLS

By FRANK LOESSER

49

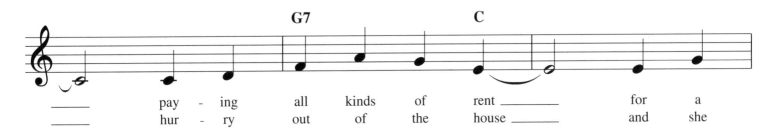

pay - ing   all   kinds   of   rent _____   for   a
hur - ry   out   of   the   house _____   and   she

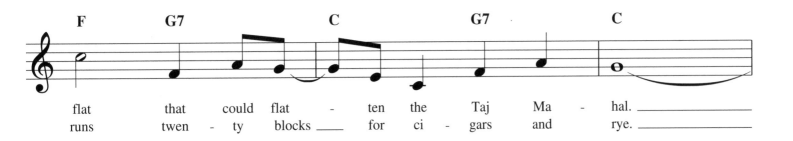

flat   that   could flat - ten   the   Taj   Ma - hal. _____
runs   twen - ty blocks ____ for ci - gars and   rye. _____

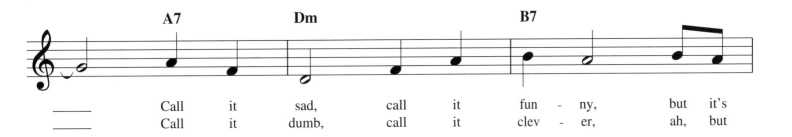

_____ Call   it   sad,   call   it   fun - ny,   but it's
_____ Call   it   dumb, call   it clev - er,   ah, but

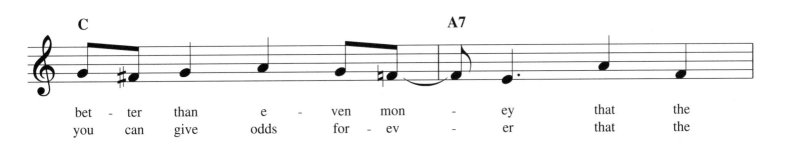

bet - ter than   e - ven mon - ey   that the
you can give   odds for - ev - er   that the

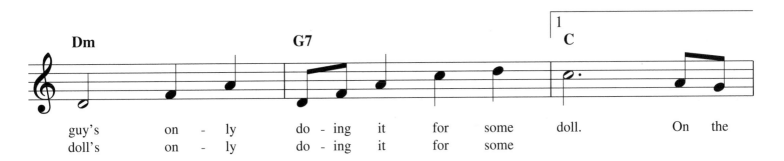

guy's   on - ly   do - ing it   for   some   doll.   On the
doll's on - ly   do - ing it   for   some

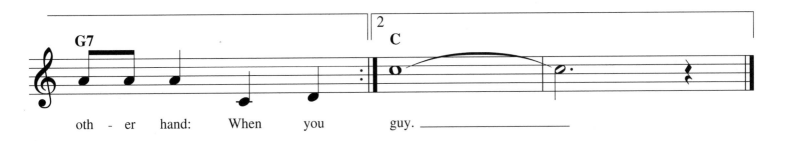

oth - er hand: When you   guy. _____

HEAT WAVE

from the Stage Production AS THOUSANDS CHEER

Words and Music by
IRVING BERLIN

51

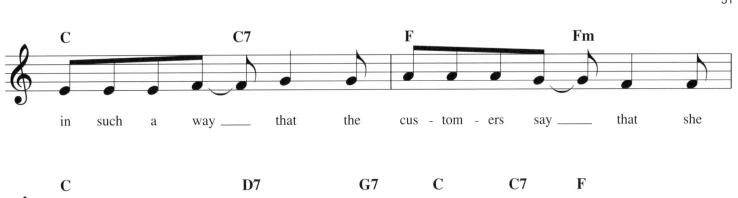

in such a way ___ that the cus - tom - ers say ___ that she

cer - tain - ly can ___ can - can. Gee _____

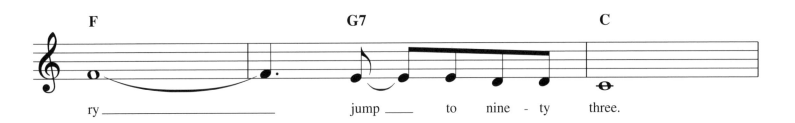

___ her ___ a - na - to - my _____ made ___ the mer - cu -

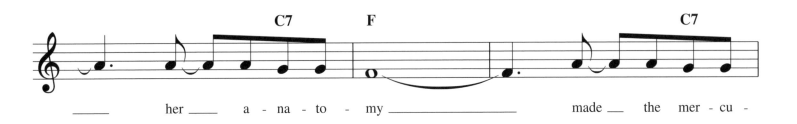

ry _____ jump ___ to nine - ty three.

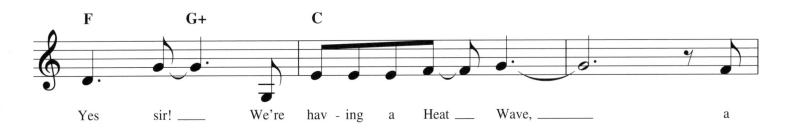

Yes sir! ___ We're hav - ing a Heat ___ Wave, _____ a

trop - i - cal Heat ___ Wave. _____ The way that she moves ___ that ther -

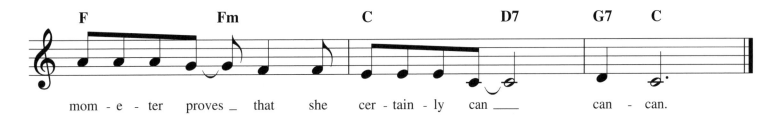

mom - e - ter proves ___ that she cer - tain - ly can ___ can - can.

HELLO, DOLLY!
from HELLO, DOLLY!

Music and Lyric by
JERRY HERMAN

I DREAMED A DREAM
from LES MISÉRABLES

Music by CLAUDE-MICHEL SCHÖNBERG
Lyrics by HERBERT KRETZMER
Original Text by ALAIN BOUBLIL and JEAN-MARC NATEL

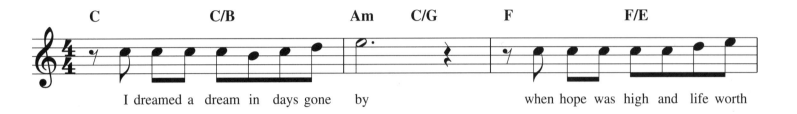

I dreamed a dream in days gone by   when hope was high and life worth

liv - ing. _____   I dreamed that love would nev - er die.

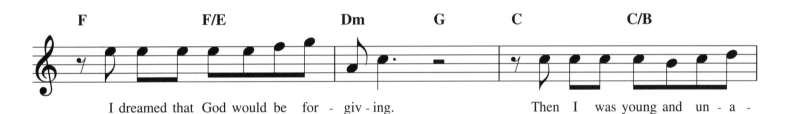

I dreamed that God would be for - giv - ing.   Then I was young and un - a -

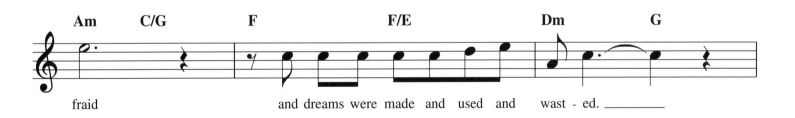

fraid   and dreams were made and used and   wast - ed. _____

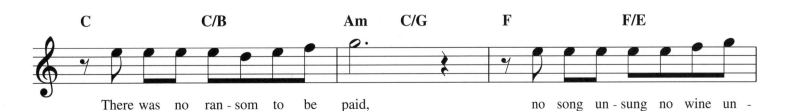

There was no ran - som to be paid,   no song un - sung no wine un -

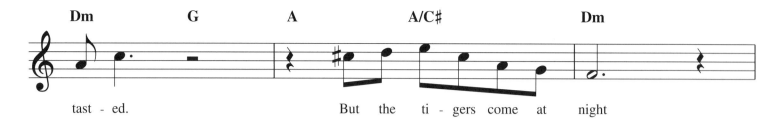

tast - ed.   But the   ti - gers come at   night

with their voic - es soft as   thun - der.   As they tear your hope a -

part,   as they turn your dream to   shame. _____

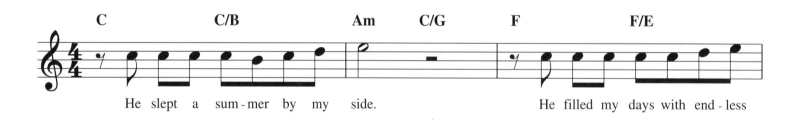

He slept a sum - mer by my side.   He filled my days with end - less

won - der.   He took my child - hood in his stride.

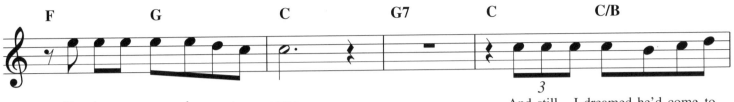

But he was gone when au-tumn came. And still I dreamed he'd come to

me, that we would live the years to - geth - er.

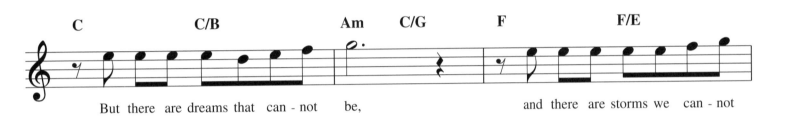

But there are dreams that can - not be, and there are storms we can - not

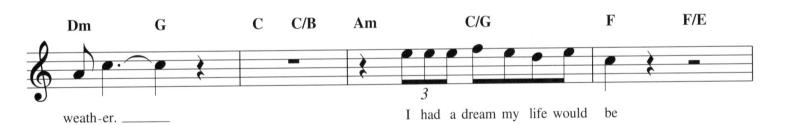

weath-er. _____ I had a dream my life would be

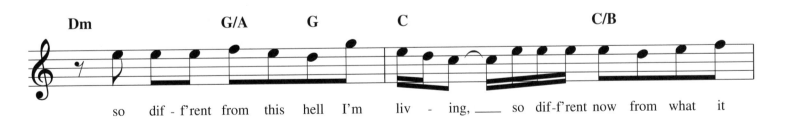

so dif - f'rent from this hell I'm liv - ing, ____ so dif-f'rent now from what it

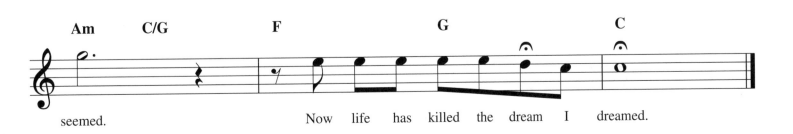

seemed. Now life has killed the dream I dreamed.

HELLO, YOUNG LOVERS
from THE KING AND I

Lyrics by OSCAR HAMMERSTEIN II
Music by RICHARD RODGERS

street in a trance. _____ You fly down a street on a

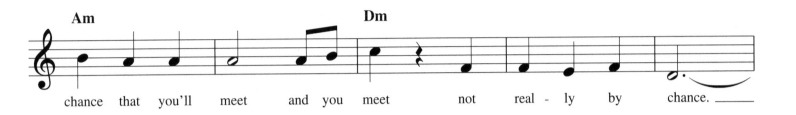

chance that you'll meet and you meet not real - ly by chance. _____

_____ Don't cry young lov - ers, what - ev - er you do, don't

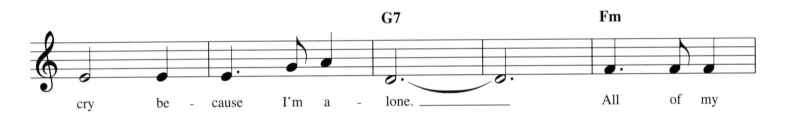

cry be - cause I'm a - lone. _____ All of my

mem - 'ries are hap - py to - night, I've had a love of my

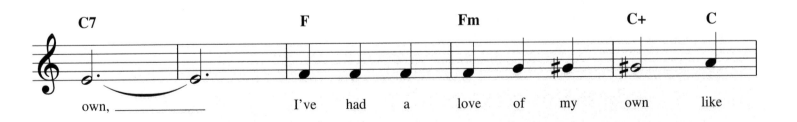

own, _____ I've had a love of my own like

yours, I've had a love of my own. _____

HOW ARE THINGS IN GLOCCA MORRA
from FINIAN'S RAINBOW

Words by E.Y. HARBURG
Music by BURTON LANE

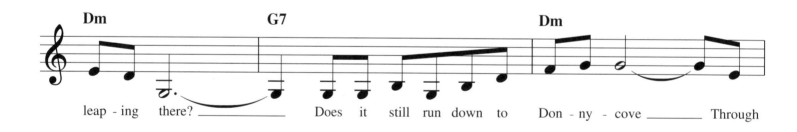

How are things in Gloc - ca Mor - ra? _____ Is that lit - tle brook still

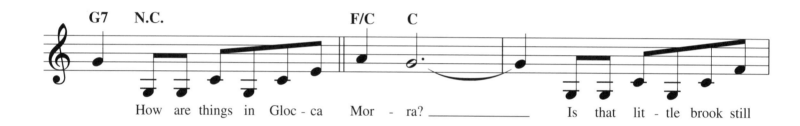

leap - ing there? _____ Does it still run down to Don - ny - cove _____ Through

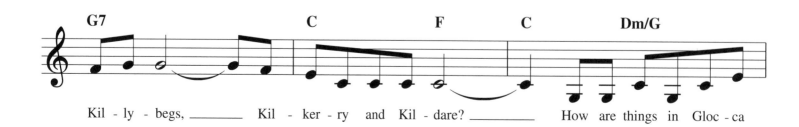

Kil - ly - begs, _____ Kil - ker - ry and Kil - dare? _____ How are things in Gloc - ca

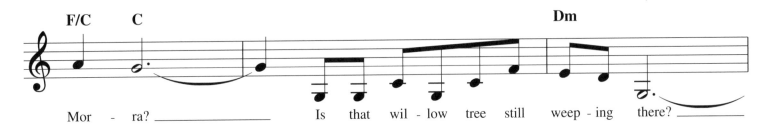

Mor - ra? _____ Is that wil - low tree still weep - ing there? _____

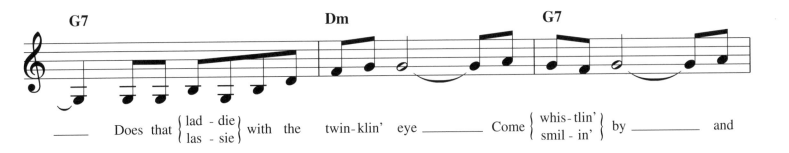

_____ Does that { lad - die / las - sie } with the twin - klin' eye _____ Come { whis - tlin' / smil - in' } by _____ and

does { he / she } walk a - way, Sad and dream - y there not to see me there? _____ So I

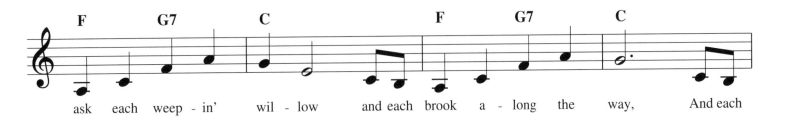

ask each weep - in' wil - low and each brook a - long the way, And each

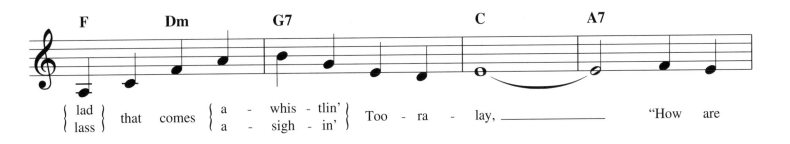

{ lad / lass } that comes { a - whis - tlin' / a - sigh - in' } Too - ra - lay, _____ "How are

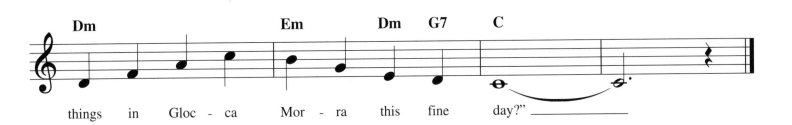

things in Gloc - ca Mor - ra this fine day?" _____

HOW DEEP IS YOUR LOVE
from the Broadway Musical SATURDAY NIGHT FEVER

Words and Music by BARRY GIBB,
MAURICE GIBB and ROBIN GIBB

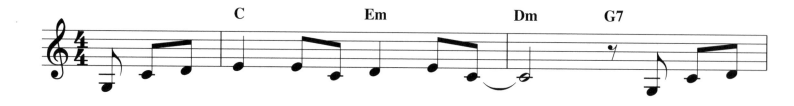

I know your eyes in the morn - ing sun. _
I be - lieve in you. _

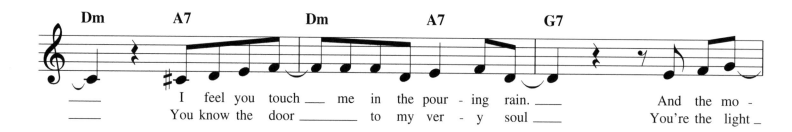

I feel you touch _ me in the pour - ing rain. _   And the mo -
You know the door _____ to my ver - y soul _   You're the light _

- ment that you wan - der far _____ from me, _____ I wan - na
_____ in my deep - est, dark - est hour: _____ you're my

feel you in my arms a - gain. _   And you come _ to me _ on a sum -
sav - ior when I fall. _   And you may _ not think _ I _ care

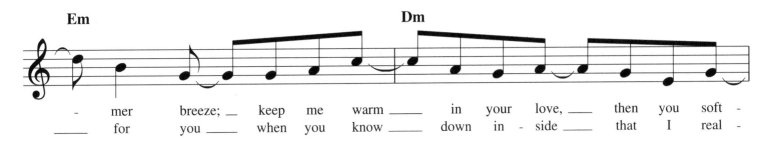

Em   Dm

- mer   breeze; _   keep   me   warm _____   in   your   love, ___   then   you   soft -
_____   for   you _____   when   you   know _____   down   in - side _____   that   I   real -

Bb7   Em   G7

- ly   leave. _ } And   it's   me   you   need _   to   show; _____   how   deep _
- ly   do. ___

C   F

_____   is   your   love? _ How   deep _____   is   your _ love?   I   real - ly   mean _   to   learn._

Fm   C   Gm   ┌─ 3 ─┐

_____   'Cause   we're   liv - ing   in   a   world   of   fools, ___   break - ing   us

A7   Dm

down   when   they   all _____   should   let   us   be. _____   We   be - long _

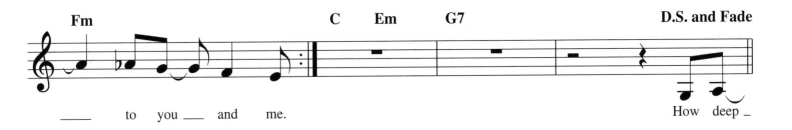

Fm   C   Em   G7   D.S. and Fade

_____   to   you _   and   me.   How   deep _

HOW TO HANDLE A WOMAN

from CAMELOT

Words by ALAN JAY LERNER
Music by FREDERICK LOEWE

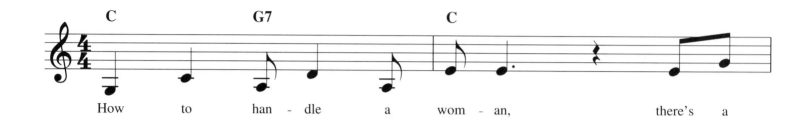

How to han-dle a wom-an, there's a

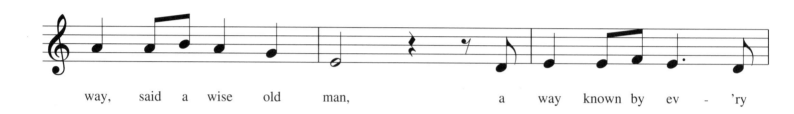

way, said a wise old man, a way known by ev-'ry

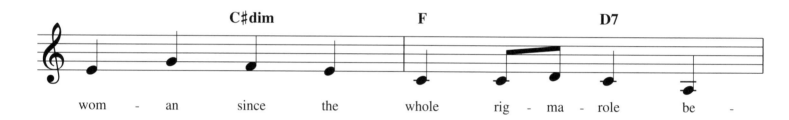

wom-an since the whole rig-ma-role be-

gan. "Do I flat-ter her?" I begged him

an-swer. "Do I threat-en or ca-jole or

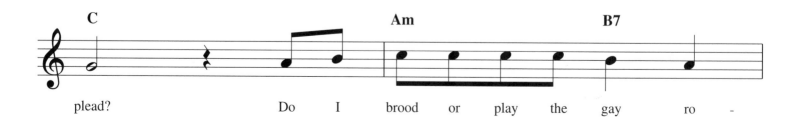

plead? Do I brood or play the gay ro-

63

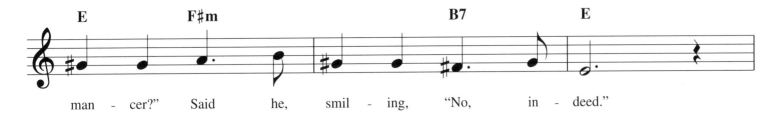

man - cer?" Said he, smil - ing, "No, in - deed."

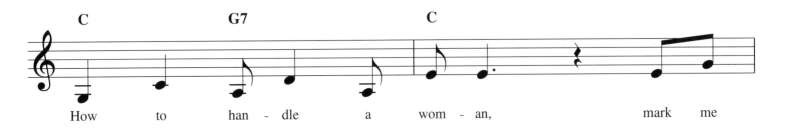

How to han - dle a wom - an, mark me

well, I will tell you, sir. "The way to han - dle a

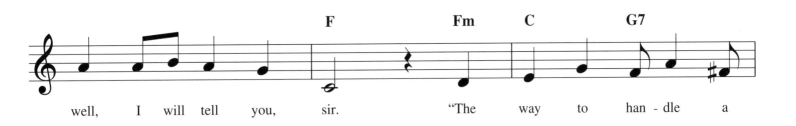

wom - an is to love her, _____ sim - ply

love her, _____ mere - ly love her,

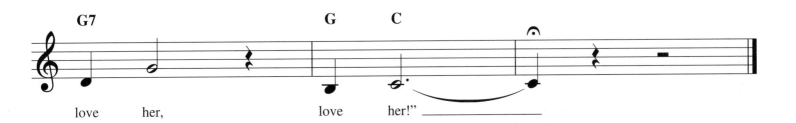

love her, love her!" _____

I AIN'T DOWN YET

from THE UNSINKABLE MOLLY BROWN

By MEREDITH WILLSON

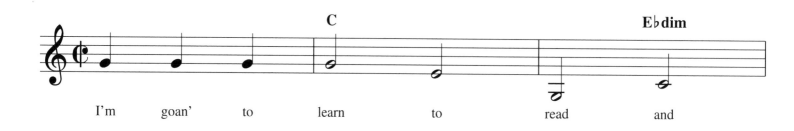

I'm   goan'   to   learn   to   read   and

write.   I'm   goan'   to   see   what   there

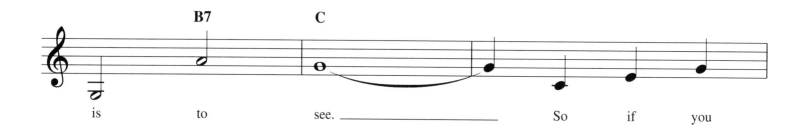

is   to   see. _____ So   if   you

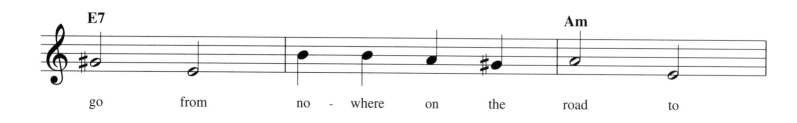

go   from   no - where   on   the   road   to

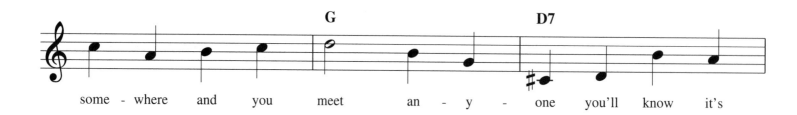

some - where   and   you   meet   an - y - one   you'll   know   it's

G   C

me.   I'm goan' to move from

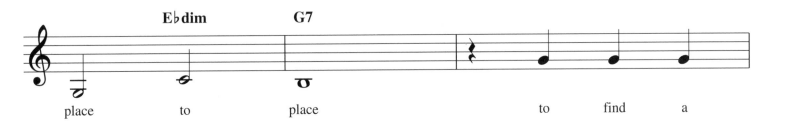

E♭dim G7

place to place   to find a

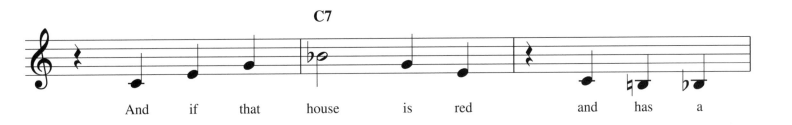

B7 C

house with a gold - en stair.

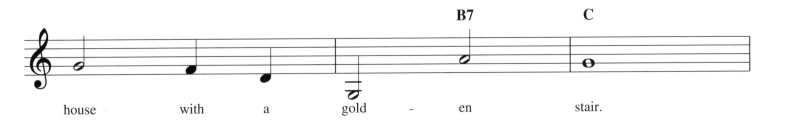

C7

And if that house is red and has a

F   Fm   C

big brass bed I'm liv -

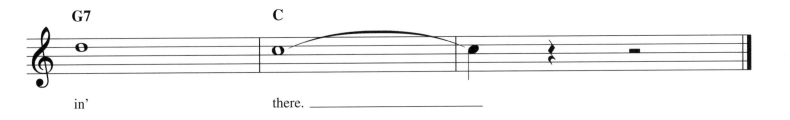

G7 C

in' there. _____

I BELIEVE IN YOU

from HOW TO SUCCEED IN BUSINESS WITHOUT REALLY TRYING

By FRANK LOESSER

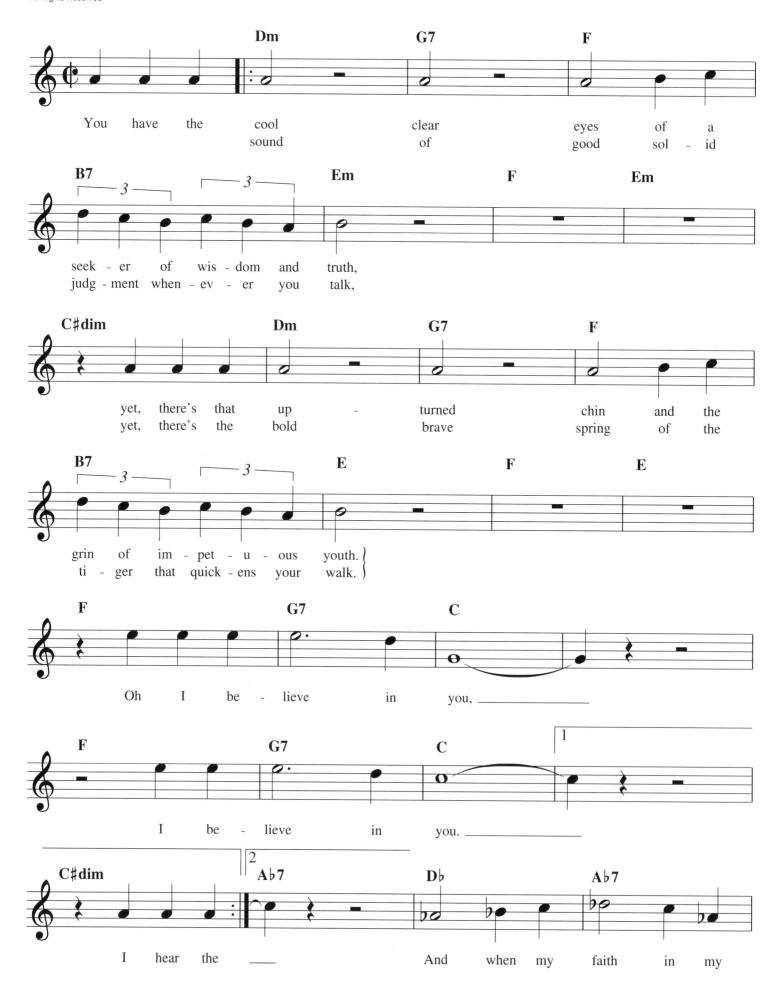

I COULD HAVE DANCED ALL NIGHT

from MY FAIR LADY

Words by ALAN JAY LERNER
Music by FREDERICK LOEWE

I could have danced all night. _____ I could have

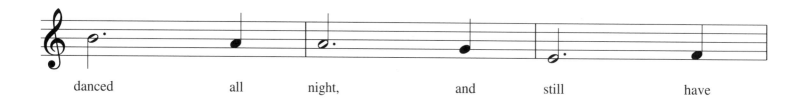

danced all night, and still have

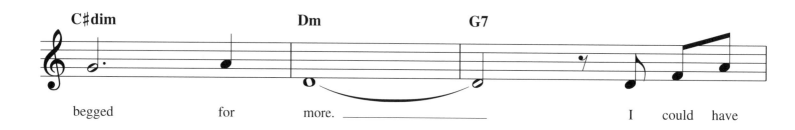

begged for more. _____ I could have

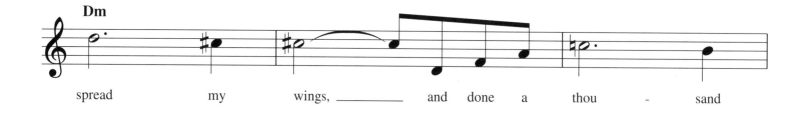

spread my wings, _____ and done a thou - sand

things I've nev - er done be -

fore. _____ I'll nev - er know _____ what made it

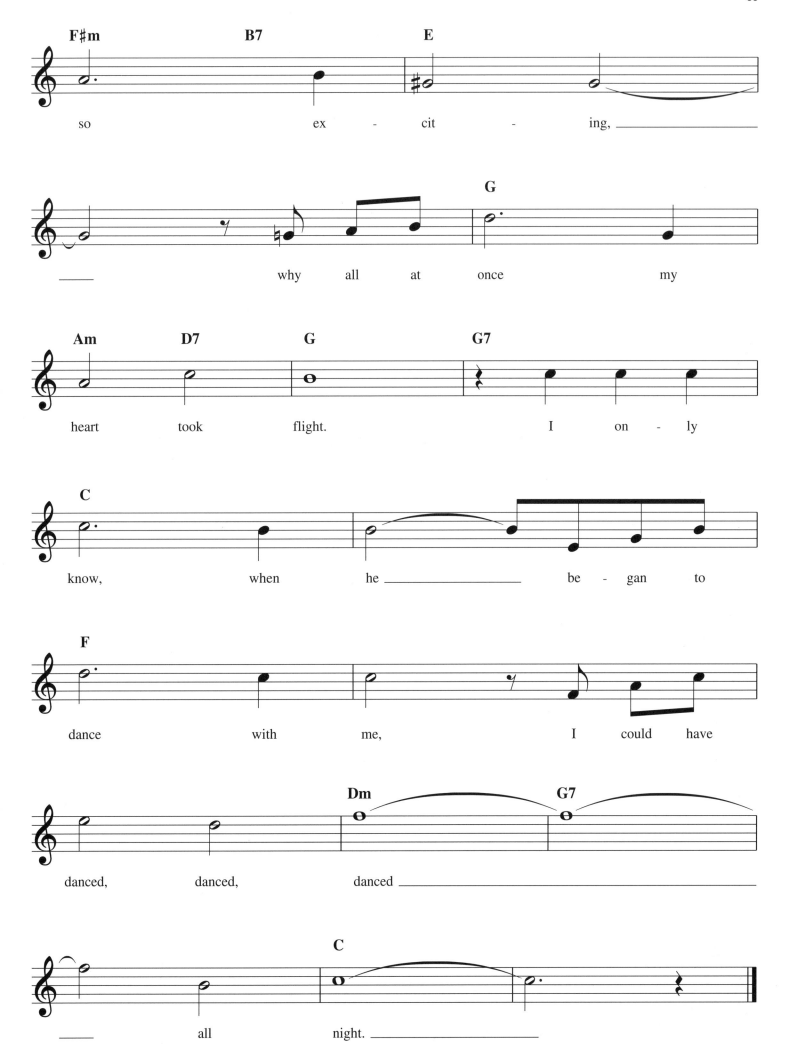

I COULD WRITE A BOOK
from PAL JOEY

Words by LORENZ HART
Music by RICHARD RODGERS

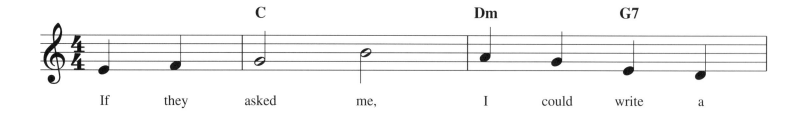

If they asked me, I could write a

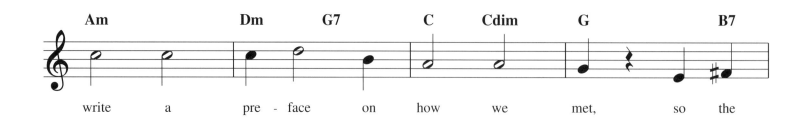

book _____ a - bout the way you walk and

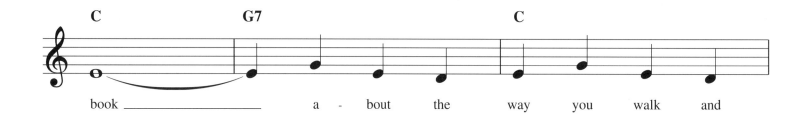

whis - per and look. I could

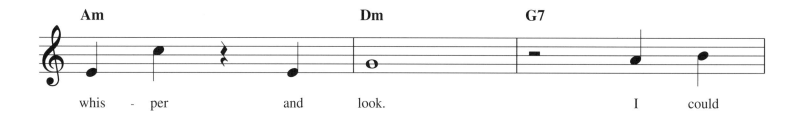

write a pre - face on how we met, so the

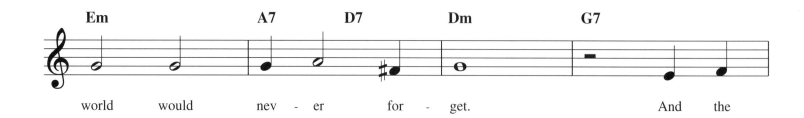

world would nev - er for - get. And the

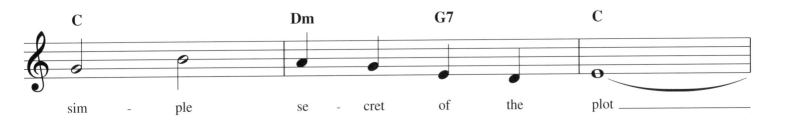

sim - ple se - cret of the plot _____

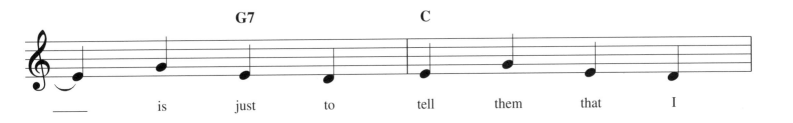

_____ is just to tell them that I

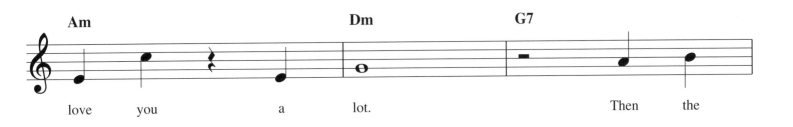

love you a lot. Then the

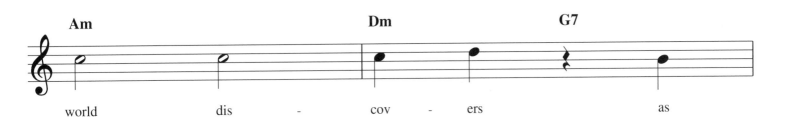

world dis - cov - ers as

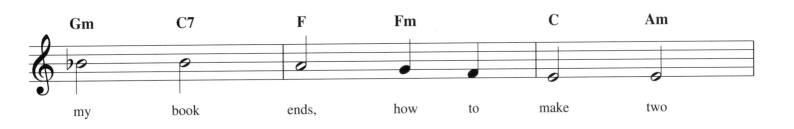

my book ends, how to make two

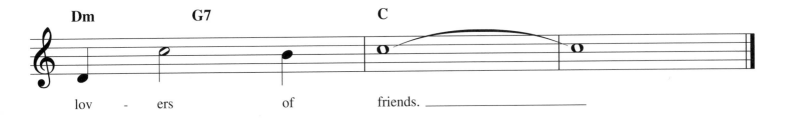

lov - ers of friends. _____

I ENJOY BEING A GIRL

from FLOWER DRUM SONG

Lyrics by OSCAR HAMMERSTEIN II
Music by RICHARD RODGERS

I HAVE DREAMED

from THE KING AND I

Lyrics by OSCAR HAMMERSTEIN II
Music by RICHARD RODGERS

I have dreamed _____ that your arms are love - ly. _____

_____ I have dreamed _____ what a joy you'll

be. _____ I have dreamed _____

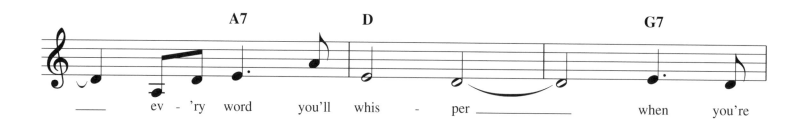

_____ ev - 'ry word you'll whis - per _____ when you're

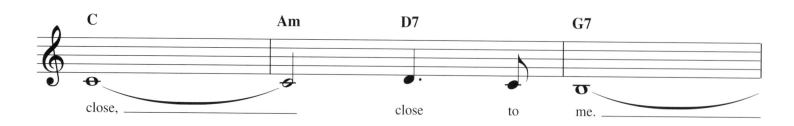

close, _____ close to me. _____

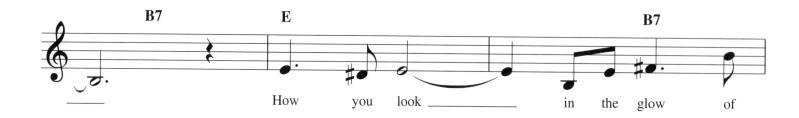

How you look _____ in the glow of

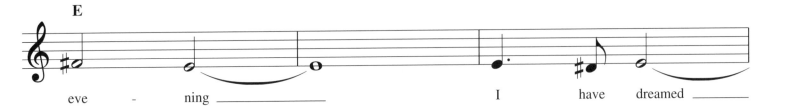

eve - ning _____ I have dreamed _____

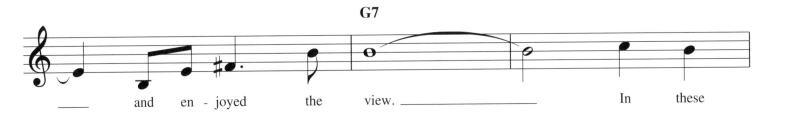

____ and en - joyed the view. _____ In these

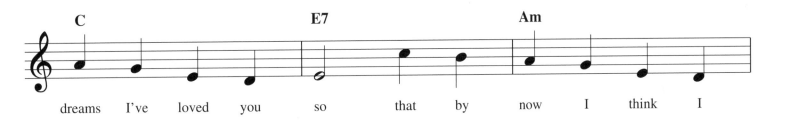

dreams I've loved you so that by now I think I

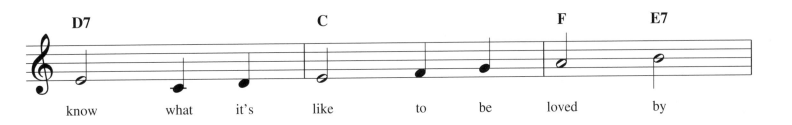

know what it's like to be loved by

you. _____ I will love be - ing

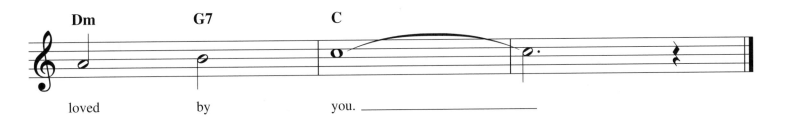

loved by you. _____

I WISH I WERE IN LOVE AGAIN
from BABES IN ARMS

Words by LORENZ HART
Music by RICHARD RODGERS

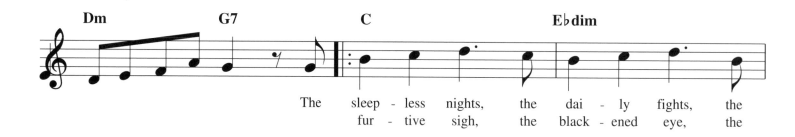

The sleep-less nights, the dai-ly fights, the
fur-tive sigh, the black-ened eye, the

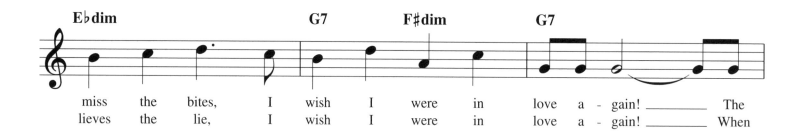

quick to-bog-gan when you reach the heights; I miss the kiss-es and I
words "I'll love you till the day I die," the self-de-cep-tion that be-

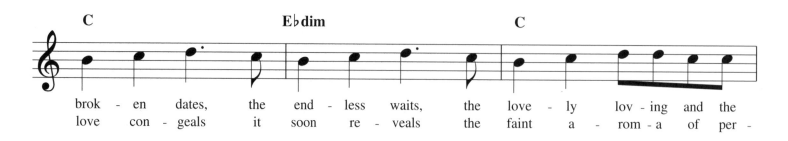

miss the bites, I wish I were in love a-gain! _____ The
lieves the lie, I wish I were in love a-gain! _____ When

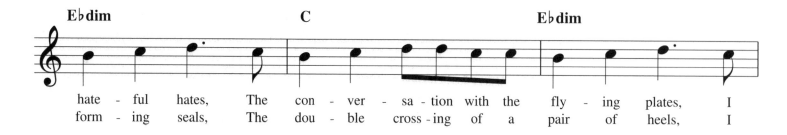

brok-en dates, the end-less waits, the love-ly lov-ing and the
love con-geals it soon re-veals the faint a-rom-a of per

hate-ful hates, The con-ver-sa-tion with the fly-ing plates, I
form-ing seals, The dou-ble cross-ing of a pair of heels, I

wish   I   were   in   love   a - gain!   No _____ more
wish   I   were   in   love   a - gain!   No _____ more

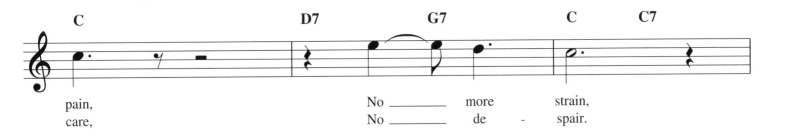

pain,   No _____ more   strain,
care,   No _____ de - spair.

Now _____ I'm   sane,   but _____   I   would rath - er   be
I'm _____ all   there   now, ___   But   I'd   rath - er   be

ga - ga! ____   The   pulled   out   fur   of   cat   and   cur,   the
punch - drunk!   Be - lieve   me   sir,   I   much   pre - fer   the

fine   mis - mat - ing   of   a   him   and   her,   I've   learned   my   les - son   but   I
clas - sic   bat - tle   of   a   him   and   her,   I   don't   like   qui - et   and   I

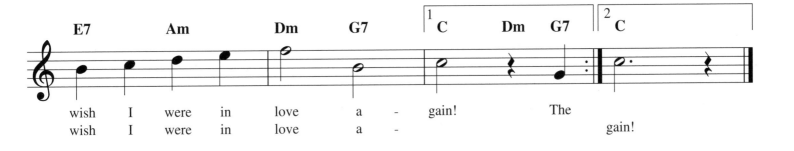

wish   I   were   in   love   a -   gain!   The
wish   I   were   in   love   a -   gain!

I WON'T SEND ROSES

from MACK AND MABEL

Music and Lyric by
JERRY HERMAN

I'LL KNOW
from GUYS AND DOLLS

By FRANK LOESSER

I'VE GROWN ACCUSTOMED TO HER FACE
from MY FAIR LADY

Words by ALAN JAY LERNER
Music by FREDERICK LOEWE

I've grown ac - cus-tomed to her face._____ She al-most makes the day be - gin._____
cus-tomed to her face._____ She al-most makes the day be - gin._____

_____ I've grown ac - cus-tomed to the tune, she whis -tles night and noon, her
_____ I've got -ten used to hear her say, "Good morn-ing" ev - 'ry day, her

smiles, her frowns, her ups, her downs are sec - ond na - ture to me now;_____
joys, her woes, her highs, her lows are sec - ond na - ture to me now;_____

_____ like breath-ing out and breath-ing in._____ I was se -
_____ like breath-ing out and breath-ing in._____ I'm ver - y

rene - ly in - de - pen - dent and con - tent be - fore we met;
grate - ful she's a wom - an and so eas - y to for - get;

sure - ly I could al-ways be that way a - gain and yet, I've grown ac - cus-tomed to her looks; ac -
rath - er like a hab - it one can al-ways break and yet, I've grown ac - cus-tomed to the trace of

cus-tomed to her voice; ac - cus-tomed to her face. I've grown ac -
some-thing in the air; ac - cus-tomed to her face.

I'VE NEVER BEEN IN LOVE BEFORE

from GUYS AND DOLLS

By FRANK LOESSER

IF HE WALKED INTO MY LIFE

from MAME

Music and Lyric by
JERRY HERMAN

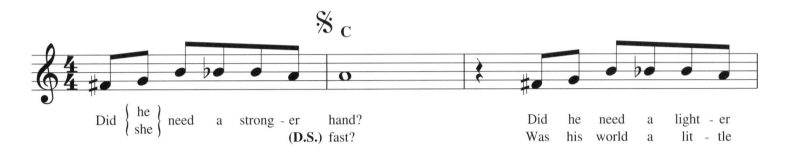

Did { he / she } need a strong-er hand? Did he need a light-er

(D.S.) fast? Was his world a lit-tle

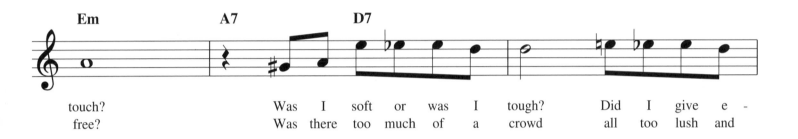

touch? Was I soft or was I tough? Did I give e-

free? Was there too much of a crowd all too lush and

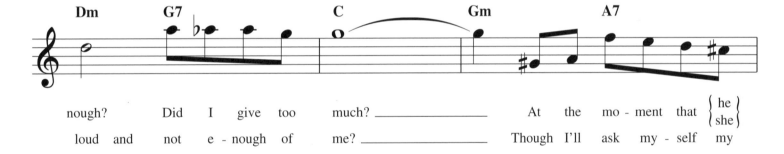

nough? Did I give too much? _____ At the mo-ment that { he / she }

loud and not e-nough of me? _____ Though I'll ask my-self my

need-ed me, _____ did I ev-er turn a-way? _____

whole life long, _____ what went wrong a-long the way. _____

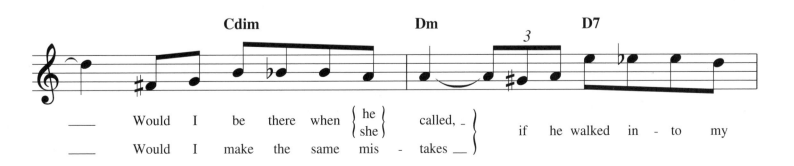

_____ Would I be there when { he / she } called, _ if he walked in-to my

_____ Would I make the same mis-takes _ }

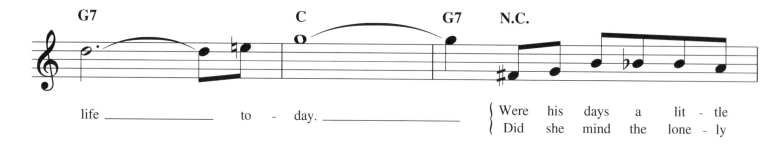

life _____ to - day. _____

{ Were his days a lit - tle
{ Did she mind the lone - ly

dull?
nights?

Were his nights a lit - tle wild?
Did she count the emp - ty days?

Did I o - ver - state my plan? Did I stress the
Was I si - lent, was I cold? Was I quick to

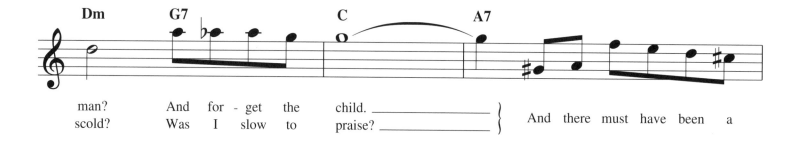

man? And for - get the child. _____ }
scold? Was I slow to praise? _____ }

And there must have been a

mil - lion things, _____ that my heart for - got to say. _____

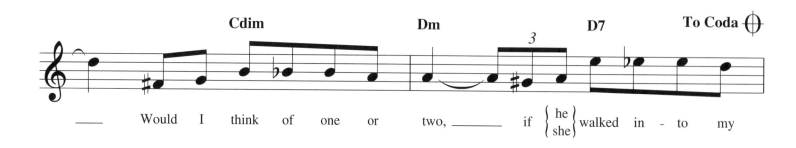

___ Would I think of one or two, _____ if { he }{ she } walked in - to my

IF EVER I WOULD LEAVE YOU

from CAMELOT

Words by ALAN JAY LERNER
Music by FREDERICK LOEWE

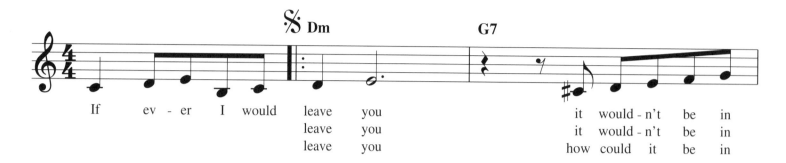

If ev - er I would leave you
it would - n't be in
leave you
it would - n't be in
leave you
how could it be in

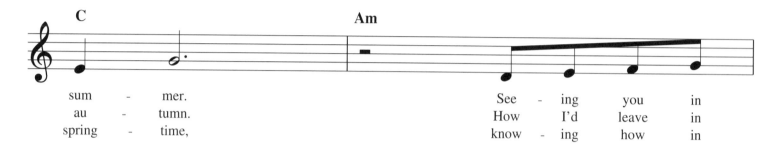

sum - mer.
See - ing you in
au - tumn.
How I'd leave in
spring - time,
know - ing how in

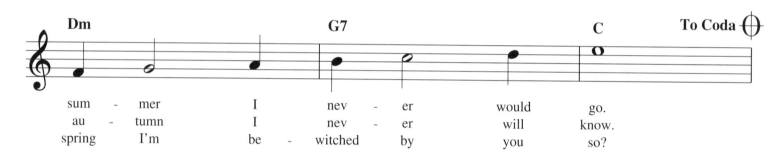

sum - mer I nev - er would go.
au - tumn I nev - er will know.
spring I'm be - witched by you so?

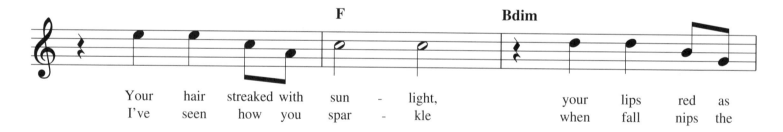

Your hair streaked with sun - light,
your lips red as
I've seen how you spar - kle
when fall nips the

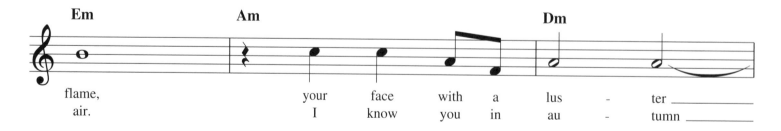

flame,
your face with a lus - ter
air.
I know with you in au - tumn

_____ that puts gold to shame. _____ But if I'd ev - er

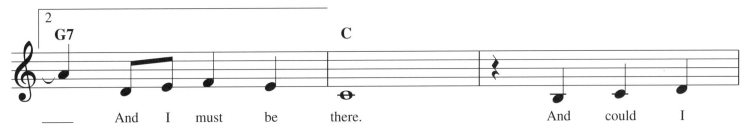

And I must be there. And could I

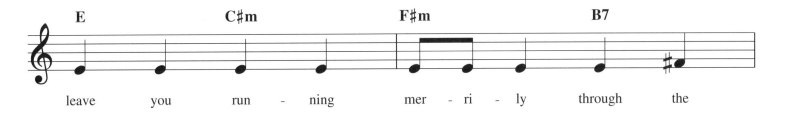

leave you run - ning mer - ri - ly through the

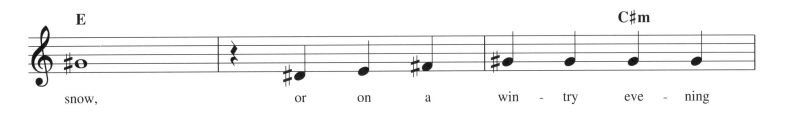

snow, or on a win - try eve - ning

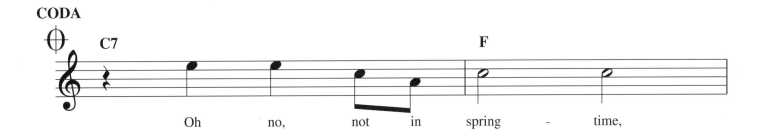

when you catch the fi - re's glow? If ev - er I would

CODA

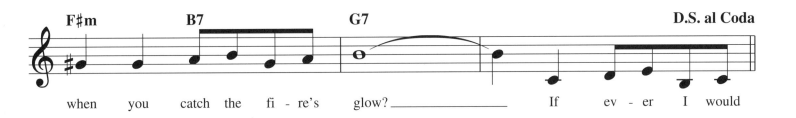

Oh no, not in spring - time,

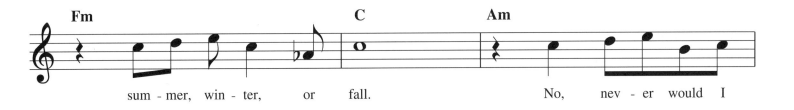

sum - mer, win - ter, or fall. No, nev - er would I

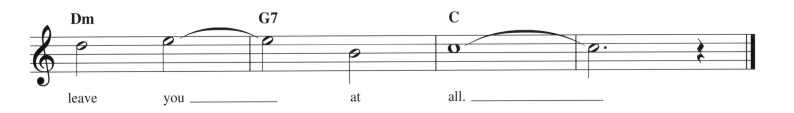

leave you at all.

IF I LOVED YOU
from CAROUSEL

Lyrics by OSCAR HAMMERSTEIN II
Music by RICHARD RODGERS

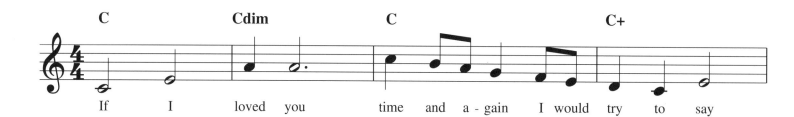

If I loved you time and a-gain I would try to say

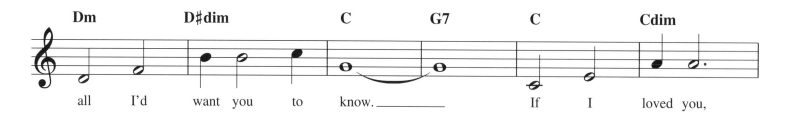

all I'd want you to know. _____ If I loved you,

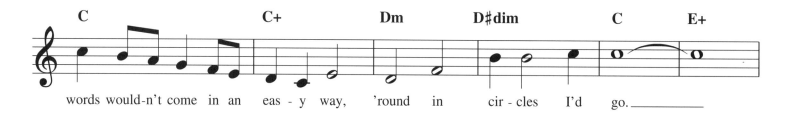

words would-n't come in an eas-y way, 'round in cir-cles I'd go. _____

Long-in' to tell you but a-fraid and shy, I'd let my

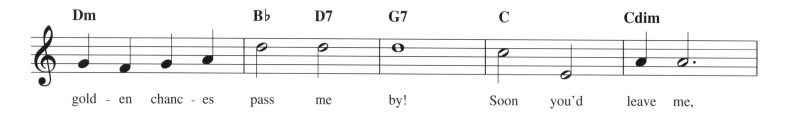

gold-en chanc-es pass me by! Soon you'd leave me,

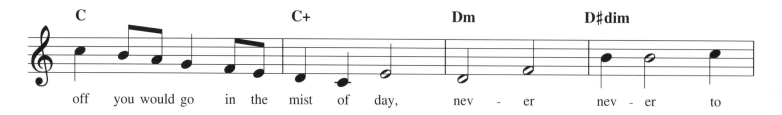

off you would go in the mist of day, nev-er nev-er to

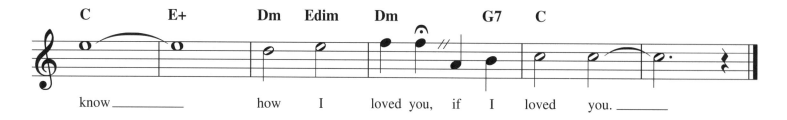

know _____ how I loved you, if I loved you. _____

LET ME ENTERTAIN YOU

from GYPSY

Words by STEPHEN SONDHEIM
Music by JULE STYNE

THE IMPOSSIBLE DREAM
(The Quest)
from MAN OF LA MANCHA

Lyric by JOE DARION
Music by MITCH LEIGH

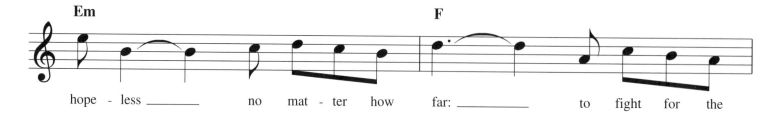

IT MIGHT AS WELL BE SPRING
from STATE FAIR

Lyrics by OSCAR HAMMERSTEIN II
Music by RICHARD RODGERS

I'm as rest-less as a wil-low in a

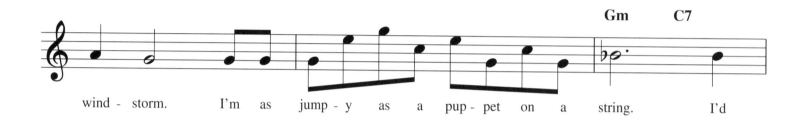

wind - storm.   I'm as jump - y as a pup - pet on a string.   I'd

say that I had spring fev - er, but I know it is - n't

spring.   I am star - ry - eyed and vague - ly dis - con - tent - ed, like a

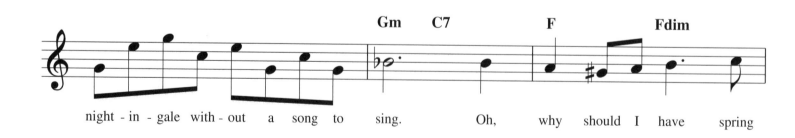

night - in - gale with - out a song to sing.   Oh, why should I have spring

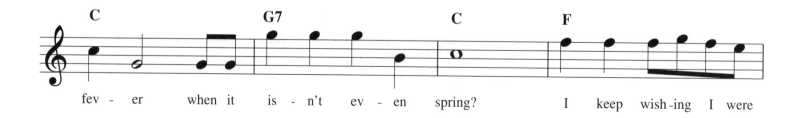

fev - er when it is - n't ev - en spring?   I keep wish - ing I were

some - where else, walk - ing down a strange new street,

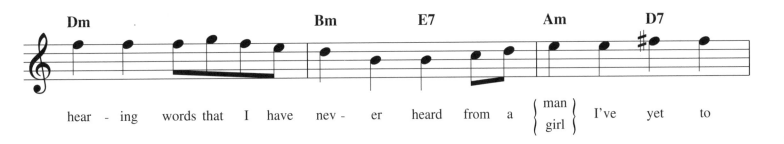

hear - ing words that I have nev - er heard from a { man / girl } I've yet to

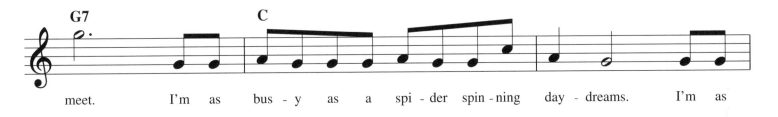

meet. I'm as bus - y as a spi - der spin - ning day - dreams. I'm as

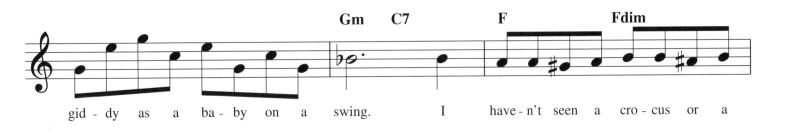

gid - dy as a ba - by on a swing. I have - n't seen a cro - cus or a

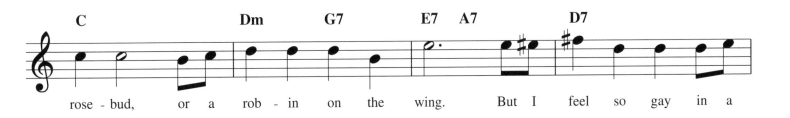

rose - bud, or a rob - in on the wing. But I feel so gay in a

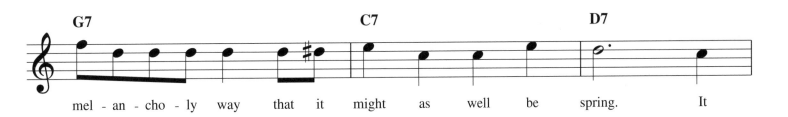

mel - an - cho - ly way that it might as well be spring. It

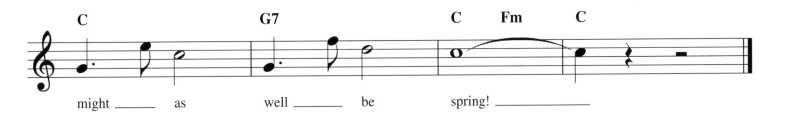

might _____ as well _____ be spring! _____

IT NEVER ENTERED MY MIND

from HIGHER AND HIGHER

Words by LORENZ HART
Music by RICHARD RODGERS

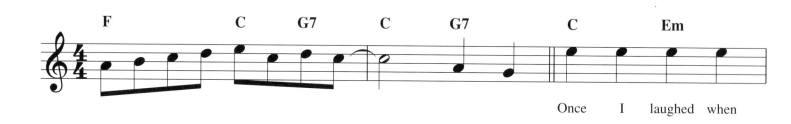

Once I laughed when

I heard you say - ing that I'd be play - ing sol - i - taire, __

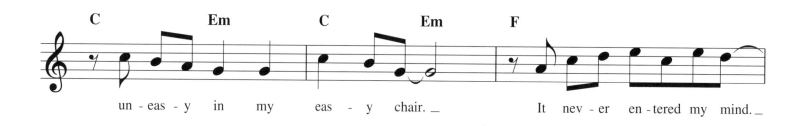

un - eas - y in my eas - y chair. __ It nev - er en - tered my mind. __

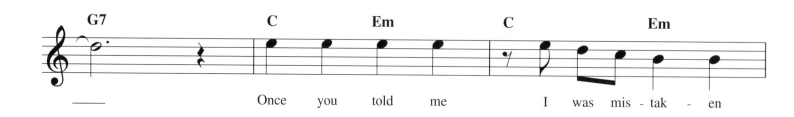

__ Once you told me I was mis - tak - en

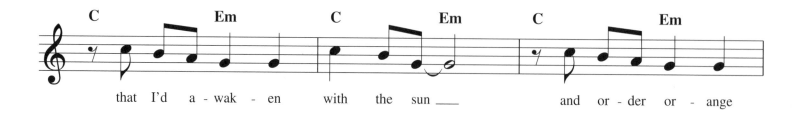

that I'd a - wak - en with the sun ___ and or - der or - ange

juice for one, ___ it nev - er en - tered my mind. ___

You have what ___ I lack my - self, ___ and now I e - ven

have to scratch my back my - self. ___ Once you warned me

that if you scorned me I'd sing the maid - en's pray'r a - gain, ___

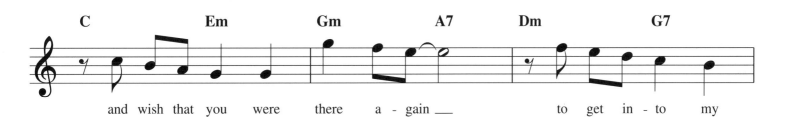

and wish that you were there a - gain ___ to get in - to my

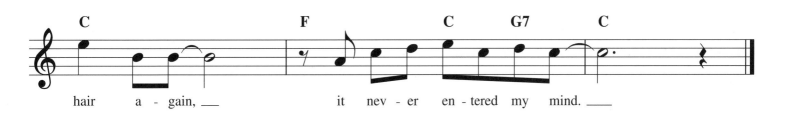

hair a - gain, ___ it nev - er en - tered my mind. ___

JUST IN TIME

from BELLS ARE RINGING

Words by BETTY COMDEN and ADOLPH GREEN
Music by JULE STYNE

Just in time _____ I found you just in time _____

_____ be - fore you came, my time _____ was run - ning

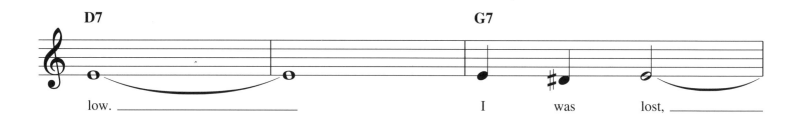

low. _____ I was lost, _____

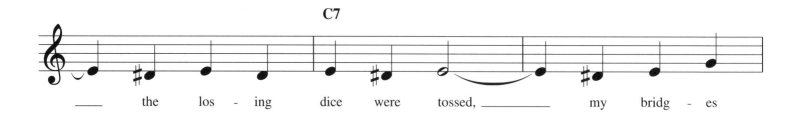

_____ the los - ing dice were tossed, _____ my bridg - es

all were crossed, _____ no - where to go. _____

Now you're here _____ and now I

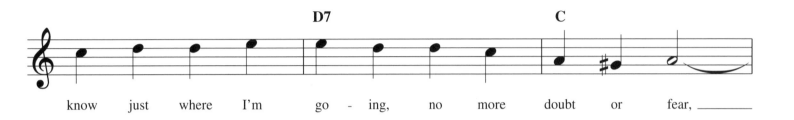

know just where I'm go - ing, no more doubt or fear, _____

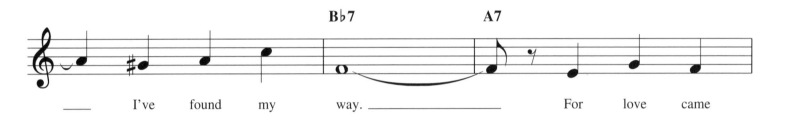

_____ I've found my way. _____ For love came

just in time. _____ You found me just in time _____

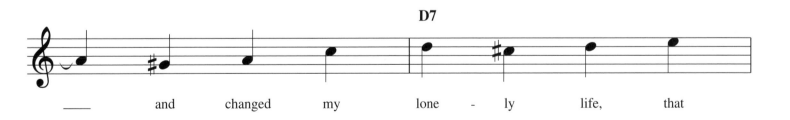

_____ and changed my lone - ly life, that

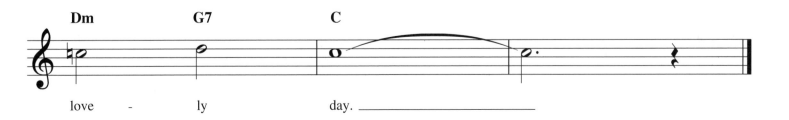

love - ly day. _____

THE LADY IS A TRAMP
from BABES IN ARMS

Words by LORENZ HART
Music by RICHARD RODGERS

I get too hun - gry for din - ner at eight, ____
I don't like crap games with bar - ons and earls. ____

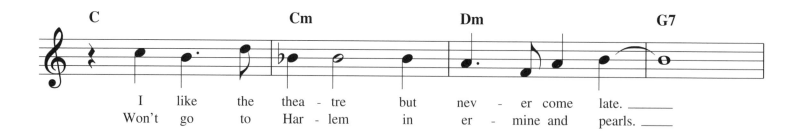

I like the thea - tre but nev - er come late. ____
Won't go to Har - lem in er - mine and pearls. ____

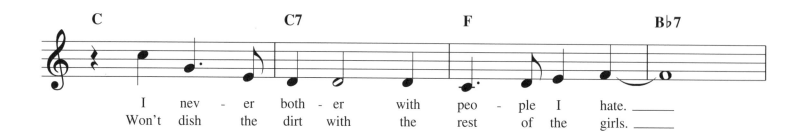

I nev - er both - er with peo - ple I hate. ____
Won't dish the dirt with the rest of the girls. ____

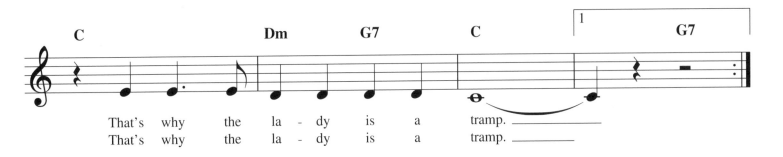

That's why the la - dy is a tramp. _____
That's why the la - dy is a tramp. _____

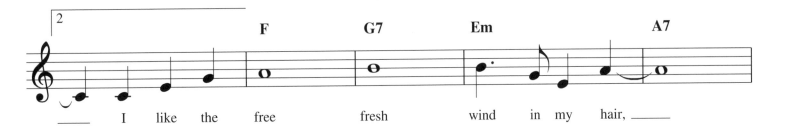

_____ I like the free fresh wind in my hair, _____

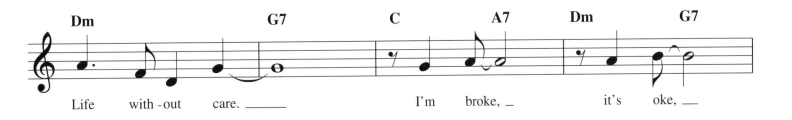

Life with -out care. _____ I'm broke, _ it's oke, _

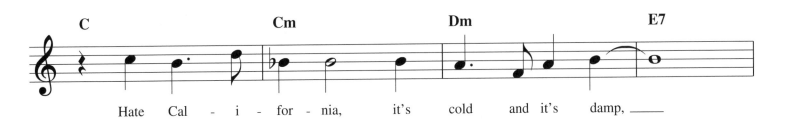

Hate Cal - i - for - nia, it's cold and it's damp, _____

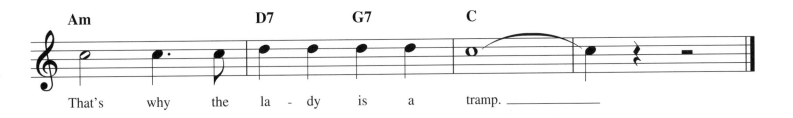

That's why the la - dy is a tramp. _____

LONG BEFORE I KNEW YOU

from BELLS ARE RINGING

Words by BETTY COMDEN and ADOLPH GREEN
Music by JULE STYNE

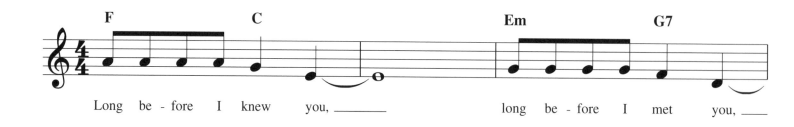

Long be-fore I knew you, _____ long be-fore I met you, _____

_____ I was sure I'd find you _____ some-day some -

how. _____ I pic - tured

some - one who'd walk and talk and smile as you do, and

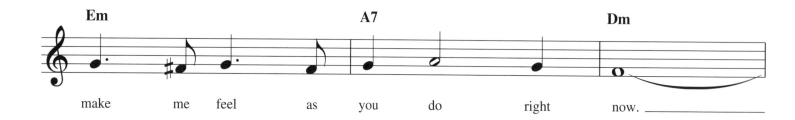

make me feel as you do right now. _____

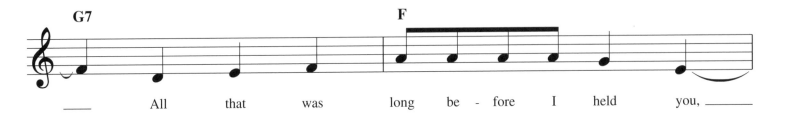

All that was long be - fore I held you, _____

_____ long be - fore I kissed you, _____

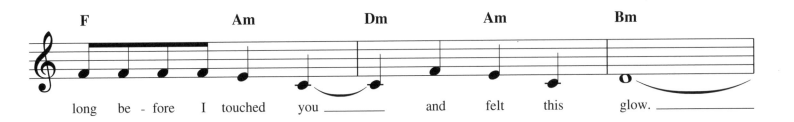

long be - fore I touched you _____ and felt this glow. _____

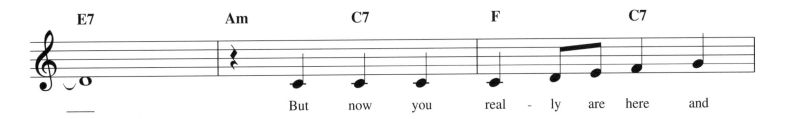

_____ But now you real - ly are here and

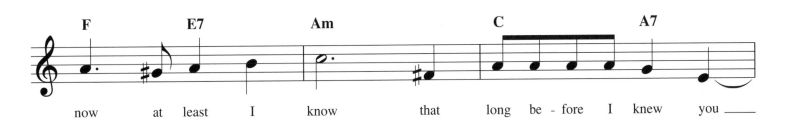

now at least I know that long be - fore I knew you _____

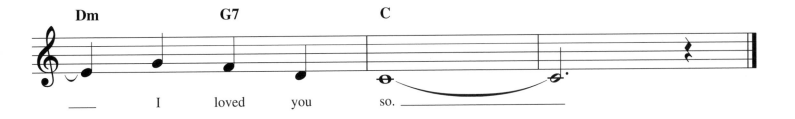

_____ I loved you so. _____

LOOK TO THE RAINBOW

from FINIAN'S RAINBOW

Words by E.Y. HARBURG
Music by BURTON LANE

LUCK BE A LADY
from GUYS AND DOLLS

By FRANK LOESSER

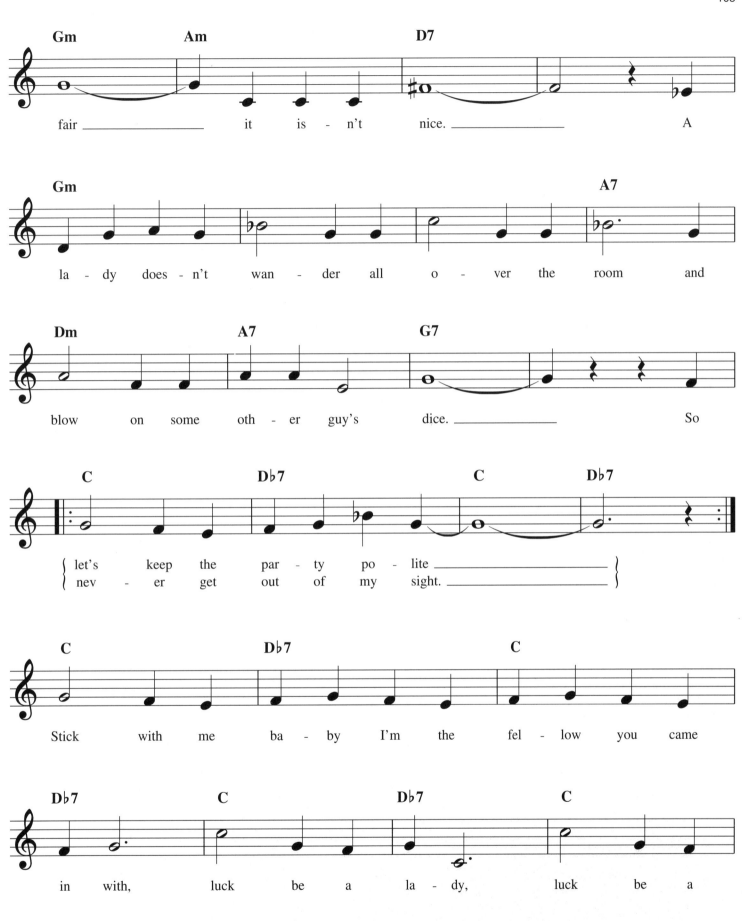

MAKE SOMEONE HAPPY

from DO RE MI

Words by BETTY COMDEN and ADOLPH GREEN
Music by JULE STYNE

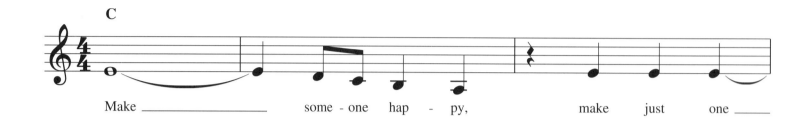

Make _____ some-one hap - py, make just one _____

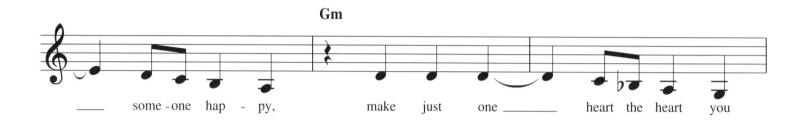

_____ some-one hap - py, make just one _____ heart the heart you

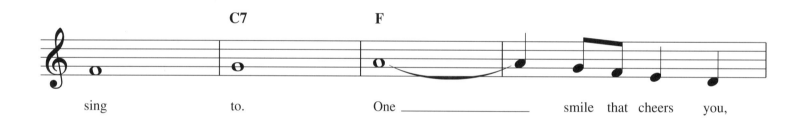

sing to. One _____ smile that cheers you,

one face that lights when it nears you, one man you're

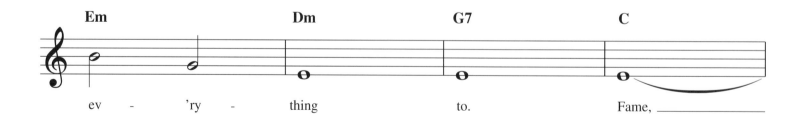

ev - 'ry - thing to. Fame, _____

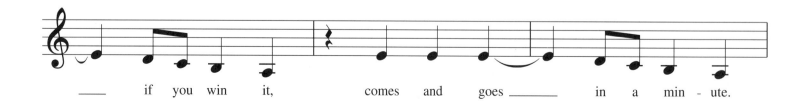

_____ if you win it, comes and goes _____ in a min - ute.

Where's the real _____ stuff in life to cling to?

Love _____ is the an - swer, some - one to

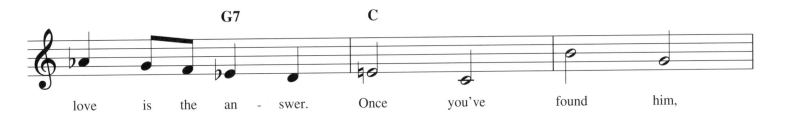

love is the an - swer. Once you've found him,

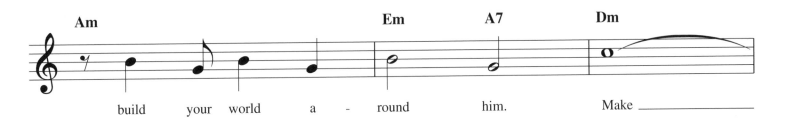

build your world a - round him. Make _____

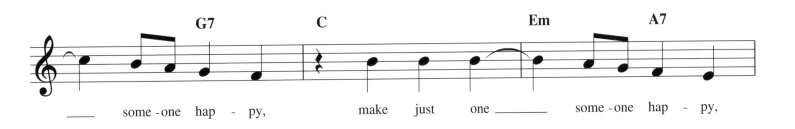

____ some -one hap - py, make just one _____ some -one hap - py,

and you _____ will be hap -py too. _____

MAME
from MAME

Music and Lyric by
JERRY HERMAN

You coax the blues right out _____ of the
You've brought the cake - walk back _____ in - to

horn, Mame. _____ You charm the
style, Mame. _____ You make the

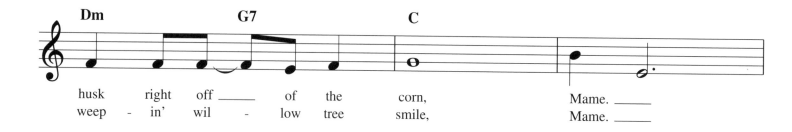

husk right off _____ of the corn, Mame. _____
weep - in' wil - low tree smile, Mame. _____

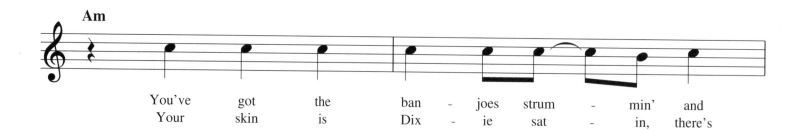

You've got the ban - joes strum - min' and
Your skin is Dix - ie sat - in, there's

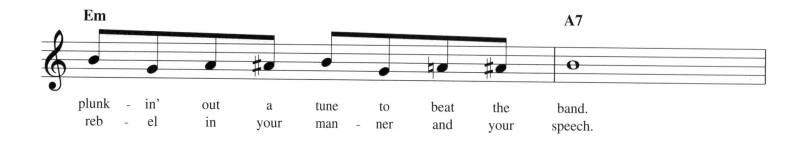

plunk - in' out a tune to beat the band.
reb - el in your man - ner and your speech.

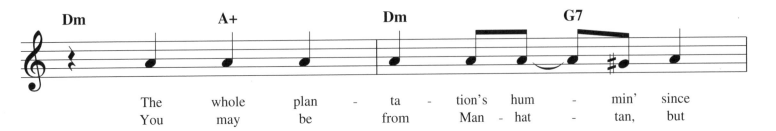

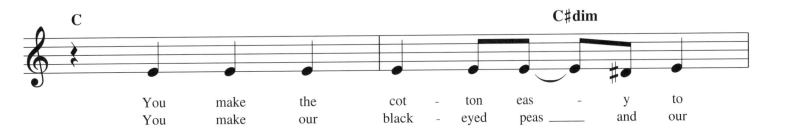

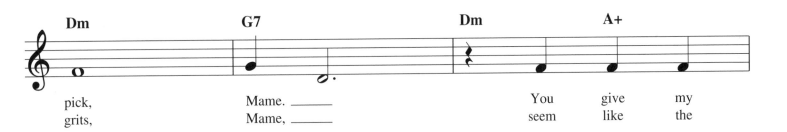

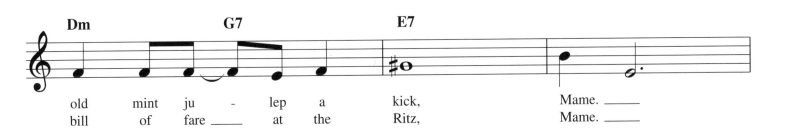

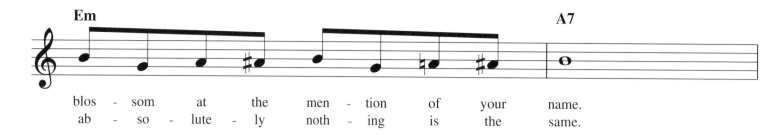

Em   **A7**

blos - som   at   the   men - tion   of   your   name.
ab - so - lute - ly   noth - ing   is   the   same.

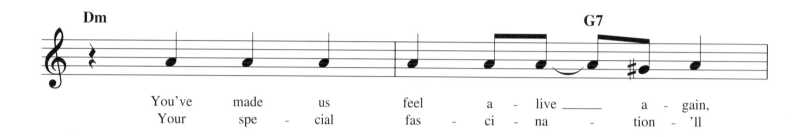

Dm   **G7**

You've made   us   feel   a - live _____ a - gain,
Your spe - cial   fas - ci - na - tion - 'll

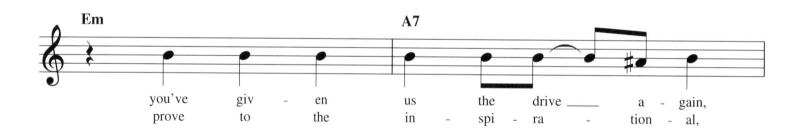

Em   **A7**

you've giv - en   us   the   drive _____ a - gain,
prove to   the   in - spi - ra - tion - al,

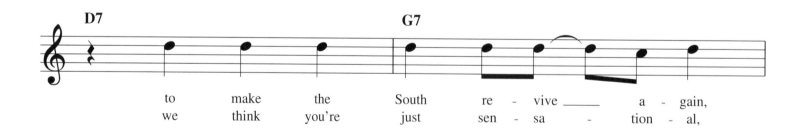

D7   **G7**

to   make   the   South   re - vive _____ a - gain,
we   think   you're   just   sen - sa - tion - al,

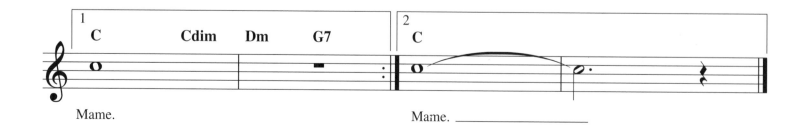

1
C   **Cdim**   **Dm**   **G7**

2
C

Mame.   Mame. _____

ME AND MY GIRL

from ME AND MY GIRL

Words by DOUGLAS FURBER and ARTHUR ROSE
Music by NOEL GAY

MAYBE
from the Musical Production ANNIE

Lyric by MARTIN CHARNIN
Music by CHARLES STROUSE

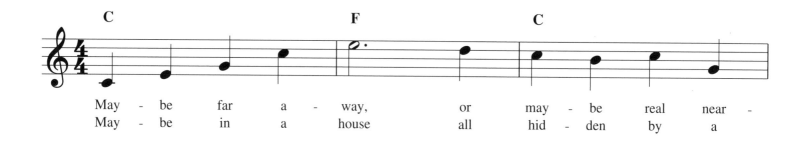

May - be far a - way, or may - be real near a -
May - be in a house all hid - den by a

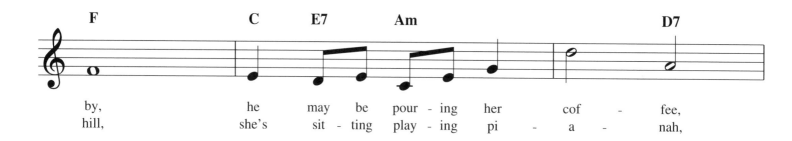

by, he may be pour - ing her cof - fee,
hill, she's sit - ting play - ing pi - a - nah,

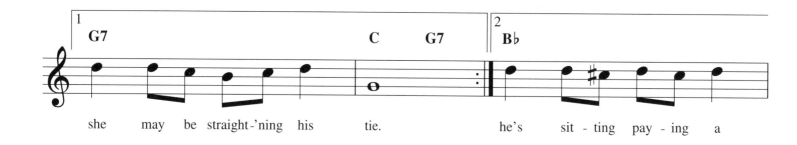

she may be straight - 'ning his tie. he's sit - ting pay - ing a

bill. Bet - cha they're young, __ bet - cha they're smart, __
Bet - cha he reads, __ bet - cha she sews, __

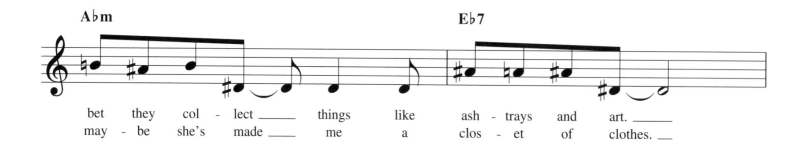

bet they col - lect ____ things like ash - trays and art. ____
may - be she's made ____ me a clos - et of clothes. ____

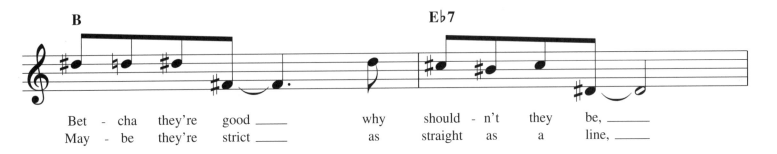

B   **E♭7**

Bet - cha they're good _____   why should - n't they be, _____
May - be they're strict _____   as straight as a line, _____

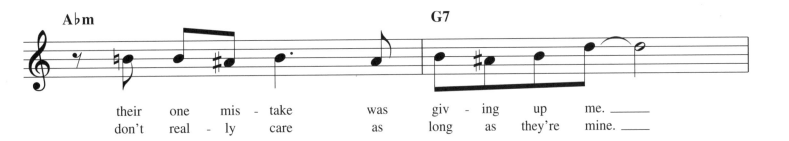

A♭m   **G7**

their one mis - take   was giv - ing up me. _____
don't real - ly care   as long as they're mine. _____

                             C   **F**

So, may - be now it's time,   and
So, may - be now this prayer's   the

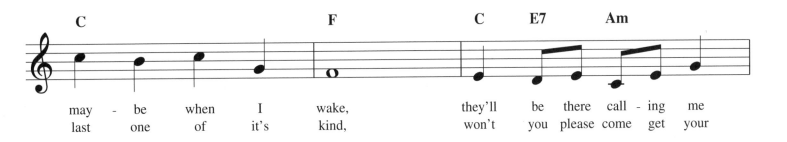

C   **F**   **C**   **E7**   **Am**

may - be when I wake,   they'll be there call - ing me
last one of it's kind,   won't you please come get your

1

        D7   **G7**   **C**   **F♯7**

"Ba - by," may - be.
ba - by,

2

G7   **C**   **F**   **C**

may - be. _____

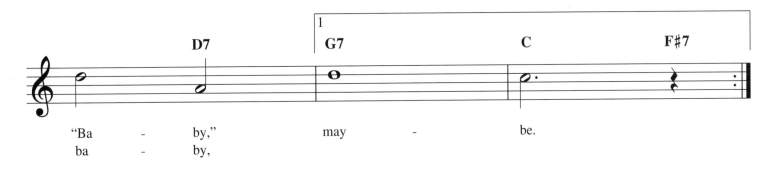

MEMORY
from CATS

Music by ANDREW LLOYD WEBBER
Text by TREVOR NUNN after T.S. ELIOT

THE MUSIC OF THE NIGHT
from THE PHANTOM OF THE OPERA

Music by ANDREW LLOYD WEBBER
Lyrics by CHARLES HART
Additional Lyrics by RICHARD STILGOE

Night time sharp-ens, height-ens each sen-sa-tion; dark-ness stirs and wakes i-mag-i-na-tion.

Si-lent-ly the sens-es a-ban-don their de-fens-es. *(Instrumental)*

Slow-ly, gen-tly, night un-furls its splen-dor;

grasp it, sense it, trem-u-lous and ten-der. Turn your face a-way from the

gar-ish light of day, turn your thoughts a-way from cold, un-feel-ing light and

lis-ten to the mu-sic of the night. Close your eyes and sur-ren-der to your

dark-est dreams! Purge your thoughts of the life you knew be-fore! Close your

117

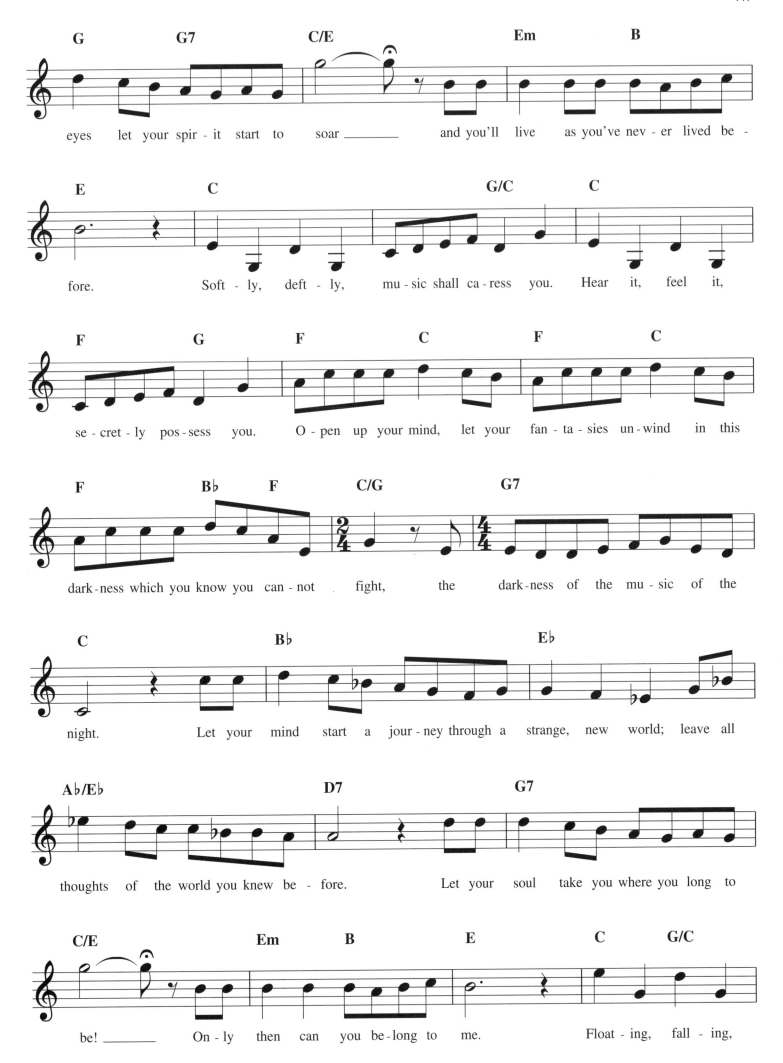

sweet in - tox - i - ca - tion. Touch me, trust me, sa - vour each sen - sa - tion.

Let the dream be - gin, let your dark - er side give in to the

pow - er of the mu - sic that I write, the pow - er of the mu - sic of the

night. *(Instrumental)*

You a - lone can make my song take flight, help me make the mu - sic of the

night. *(Instrumental)*

MY HEART STOOD STILL
from A CONNECTICUT YANKEE

Words by LORENZ HART
Music by RICHARD RODGERS

I took one look at you, that's all I meant to do,
My feet could step and walk, my lips could move and talk,

and then my heart stood still!
and yet my heart stood still! Though not a

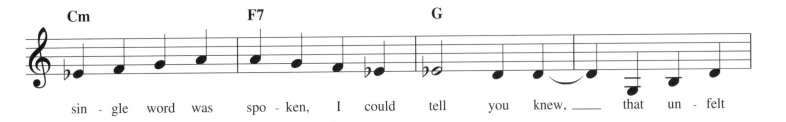

sin - gle word was spo - ken, I could tell you knew, ___ that un - felt

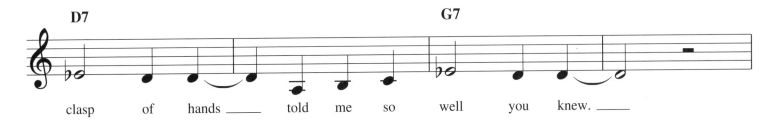

clasp of hands ___ told me so well you knew. ___

I nev - er lived at all un - til the thrill of that

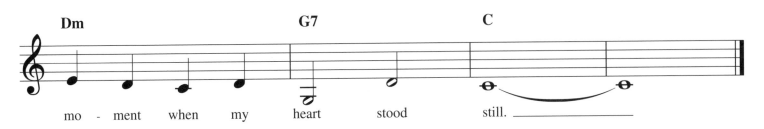

mo - ment when my heart stood still. ___

MY FAVORITE THINGS
from THE SOUND OF MUSIC

Lyrics by OSCAR HAMMERSTEIN II
Music by RICHARD RODGERS

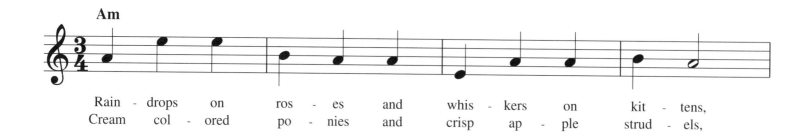

Rain - drops   on   ros - es   and   whis - kers   on   kit - tens,
Cream col - ored   po - nies   and   crisp   ap - ple   strud - els,

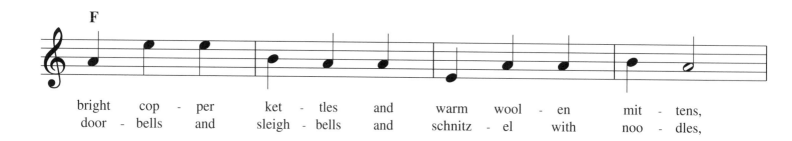

bright   cop - per   ket - tles   and   warm   wool - en   mit - tens,
door - bells   and   sleigh - bells   and   warm   schnitz - el   with   noo - dles,

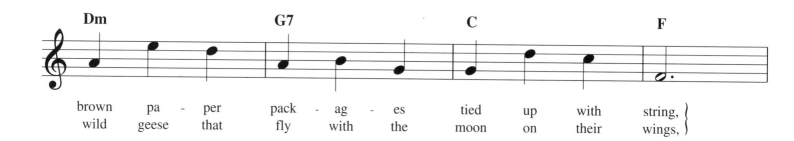

brown   pa - per   pack - ag - es   tied   up   with   string, }
wild   geese   that   fly   with   the   moon   on   their   wings, }

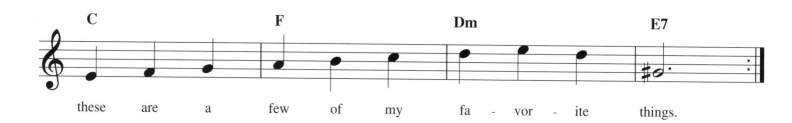

these   are   a   few   of   my   fa - vor - ite   things.

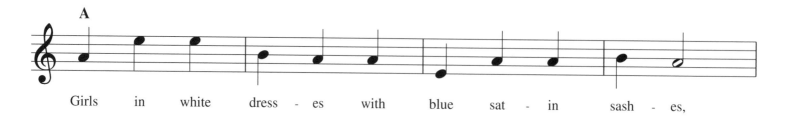

Girls   in   white   dress - es   with   blue   sat - in   sash - es,

snow - flakes   that   stay   on   my   nose   and   eye - lash - es,

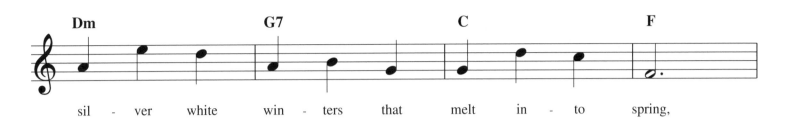

sil - ver white win - ters that melt in - to spring,

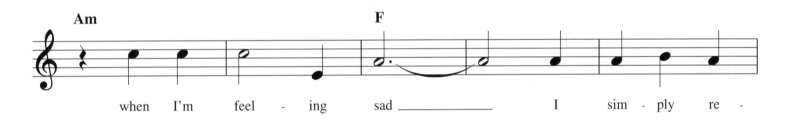

these are a few of my fa - vor - ite things.

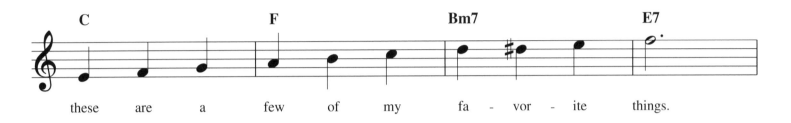

When the dog bites, when the bee stings,

when I'm feel - ing sad _____ I sim - ply re -

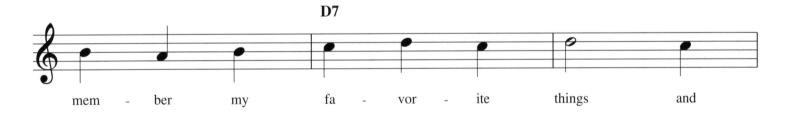

mem - ber my fa - vor - ite things and

then I don't feel so

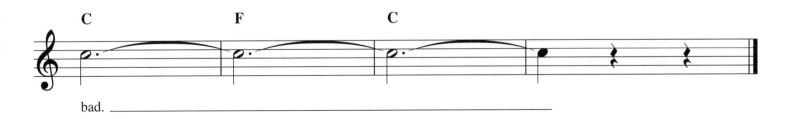

bad. _____

MY FUNNY VALENTINE

from BABES IN ARMS

Words by LORENZ HART
Music by RICHARD RODGERS

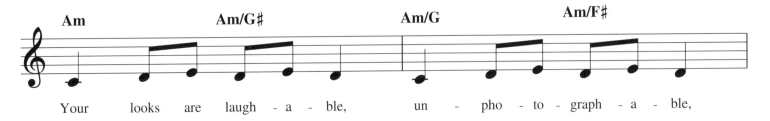

Your looks are laugh - a - ble, un - pho - to - graph - a - ble,

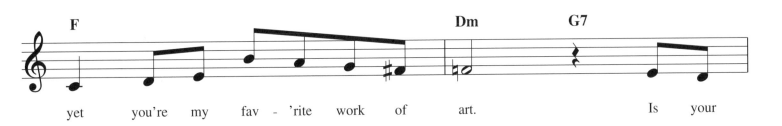

yet you're my fav - 'rite work of art. Is your

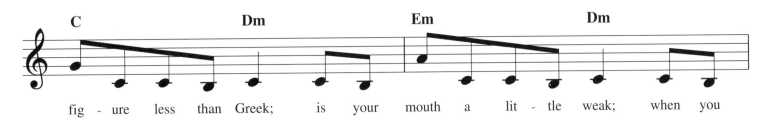

fig - ure less than Greek; is your mouth a lit - tle weak; when you

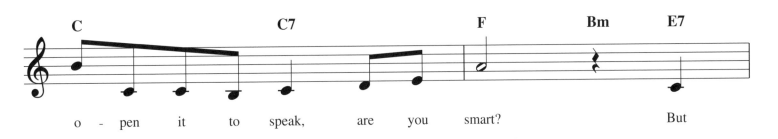

o - pen it to speak, are you smart? But

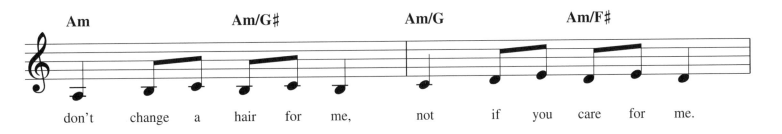

don't change a hair for me, not if you care for me.

Stay, lit - tle Val - en - tine, stay.

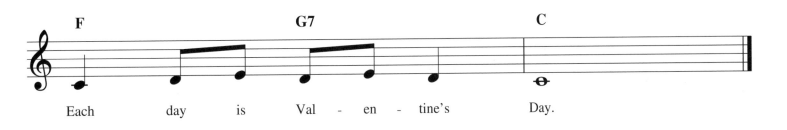

Each day is Val - en - tine's Day.

MY ROMANCE
from JUMBO

Words by LORENZ HART
Music by RICHARD RODGERS

NO OTHER LOVE
from ME AND JULIET

Lyrics by OSCAR HAMMERSTEIN II
Music by RICHARD RODGERS

OH, WHAT A BEAUTIFUL MORNIN'
from OKLAHOMA!

Lyrics by OSCAR HAMMERSTEIN II
Music by RICHARD RODGERS

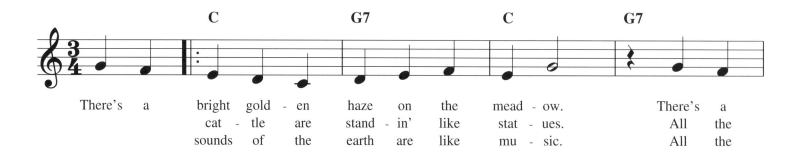

There's a bright gold - en haze on the mead - ow. There's a
cat - tle are stand - in' like stat - ues. All the
sounds of the earth are like mu - sic. All the

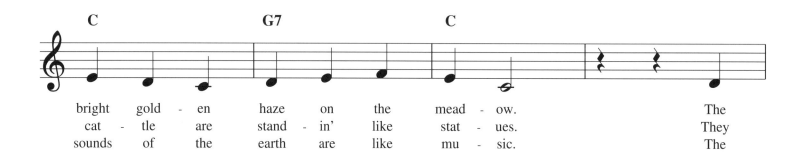

bright gold - en haze on the mead - ow. The
cat - tle are stand - in' like stat - ues. They
sounds of the earth are like mu - sic. The

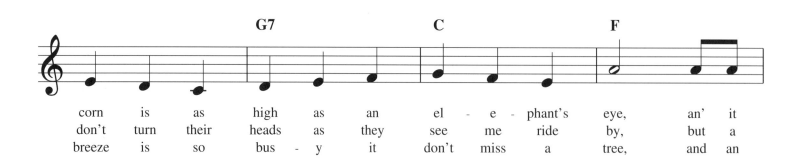

corn is as high as an el - e - phant's eye, an' it
don't turn their heads as they see me ride by, but a
breeze is so bus - y it don't miss a tree, and an

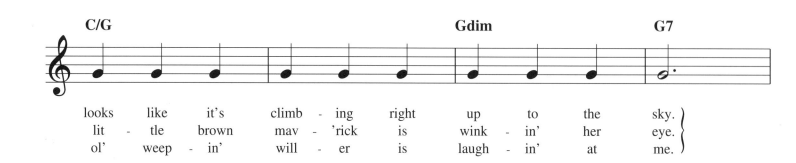

looks like it's climb - ing right up to the sky.
lit - tle brown mav - 'rick is wink - in' her eye.
ol' weep - in' will - er is laugh - in' at me.

Oh, what a beau - ti - ful morn - in',

oh, what a beau - ti - ful day. _____

I got a beau - ti - ful feel - in'

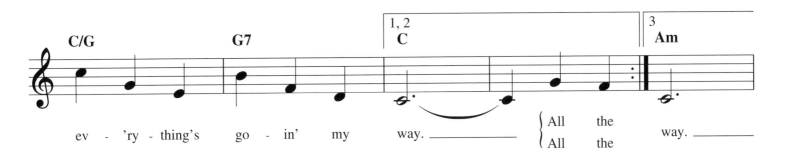

ev - 'ry - thing's go - in' my way. _____ All the way. _____
All the

Oh, what a beau - ti - ful day. _____

ON THE STREET WHERE YOU LIVE

from MY FAIR LADY

Words by ALAN JAY LERNER
Music by FREDERICK LOEWE

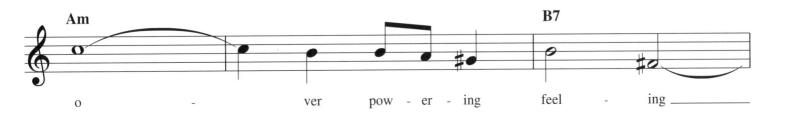

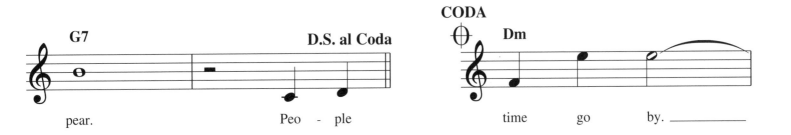

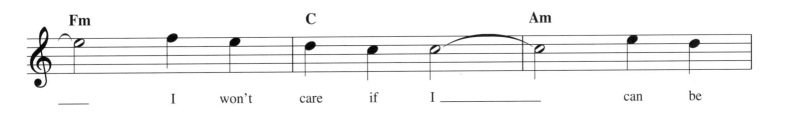

ONE

from A CHORUS LINE

Music by MARVIN HAMLISCH
Lyric by EDWARD KLEBAN

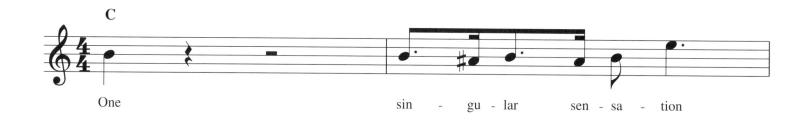

One   sin - gu - lar   sen - sa - tion

ev - 'ry lit - tle step   she   takes. _____

One   thrill - ing com - bi - na - tion

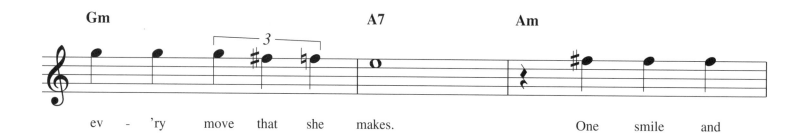

ev - 'ry move that she makes.   One smile and

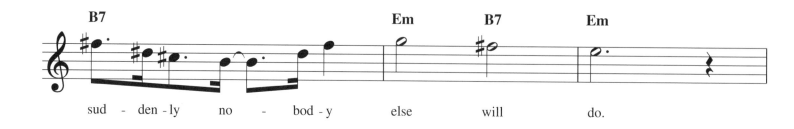

sud - den - ly no - bod - y else will do.

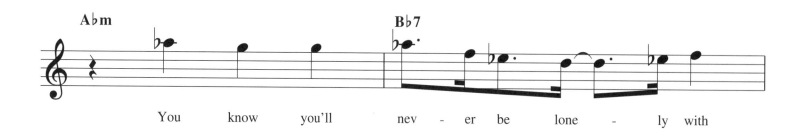

You know you'll nev - er be lone - ly with

PEOPLE
from FUNNY GIRL

Words by BOB MERRILL
Music by JULE STYNE

Peo - ple, _____ peo - ple who need peo - ple _____ are the

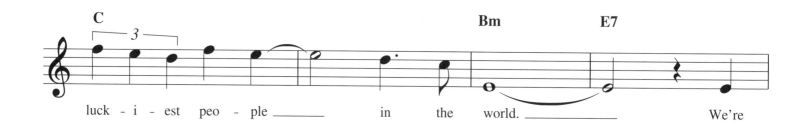

luck - i - est peo - ple _____ in the world. _____ We're

chil - dren _____ need - ing oth - er chil - dren _____ and yet

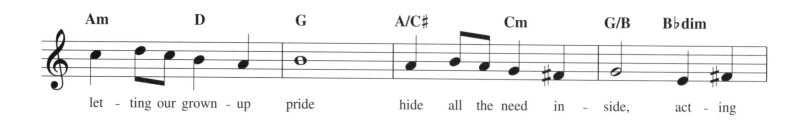

let - ting our grown - up pride hide all the need in - side, act - ing

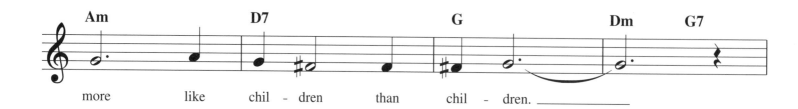

more like chil - dren than chil - dren. _____

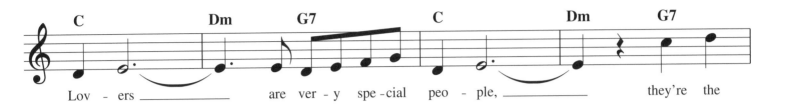

Lov - ers _____ are ver - y spe -cial peo - ple, _____ they're the

luck - i - est peo - ple _____ in the world. _____ With one

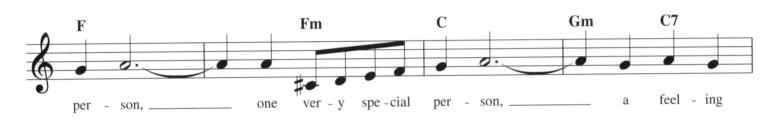

per - son, _____ one ver - y spe -cial per - son, _____ a feel - ing

deep in your soul _____ says you were half, now you're whole. _____ No more

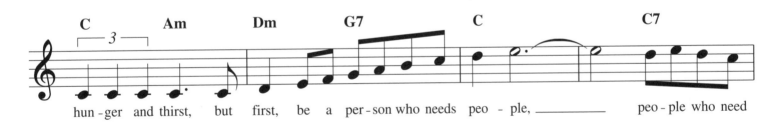

hun -ger and thirst, but first, be a per -son who needs peo - ple, _____ peo -ple who need

peo - ple _____ are the luck - i - est peo - ple in the

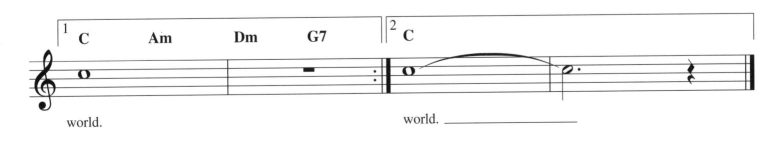

world. world. _____

PEOPLE WILL SAY WE'RE IN LOVE

from OKLAHOMA!

Lyrics by OSCAR HAMMERSTEIN II
Music by RICHARD RODGERS

Don't throw _____ bou - quets at me. _____

Don't please _____ my folks too much. _____

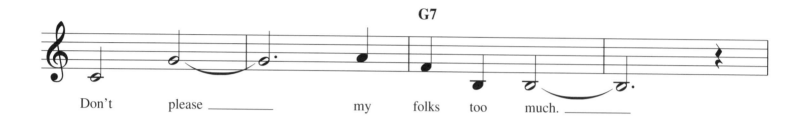

Don't laugh _____ at my jokes too much. _____

Peo - ple will say we're in love! _____

Don't sigh _____ and gaze at me. _____

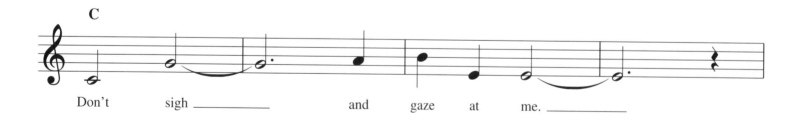

Your sighs _____ are so like mine. _____

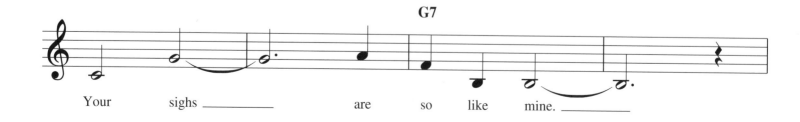

Your eyes _____ must - n't glow like mine. _____

Peo - ple will say we're in love! _____

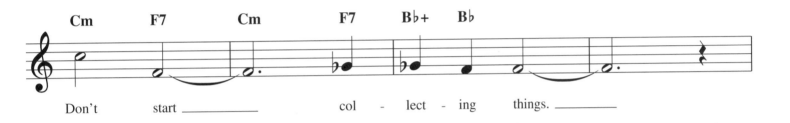

Don't start _____ col - lect - ing things. _____

Give me my rose and my glove. _____

Sweet - heart, _____ they're sus - pect - ing things. _____

Peo - ple will say we're in love. _____

PREPARE YE (THE WAY OF THE LORD)
from the Musical GODSPELL

Words and Music by
STEPHEN SCHWARTZ

THIS CAN'T BE LOVE
from THE BOYS FROM SYRACUSE

Words by LORENZ HART
Music by RICHARD RODGERS

SEASONS OF LOVE

from RENT

Words and Music by
JONATHAN LARSON

Five hun - dred twen -ty five thou - sand six hun - dred min - utes,

five hun - dred twen -ty five thou - sand mo - ments so ____ dear. ____

Five hun - dred twen -ty five thou - sand six hun - dred min - utes.

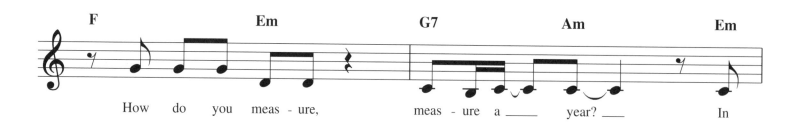

How do you meas - ure, meas - ure a ____ year? ____ In

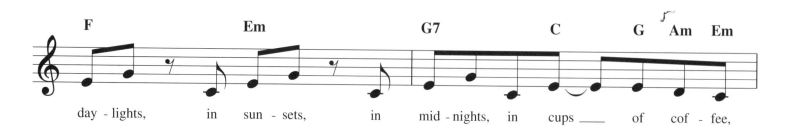

day - lights, in sun - sets, in mid - nights, in cups ____ of cof - fee,

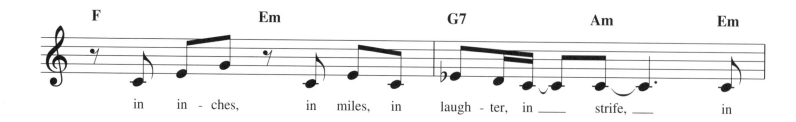

in in - ches, in miles, in laugh - ter, in ____ strife, ____ in

five hun-dred twen-ty five thou-sand six hun-dred min - utes. How

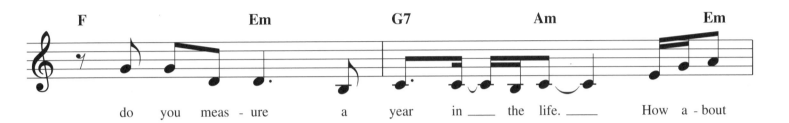

do you meas-ure a year in ___ the life. ___ How a-bout

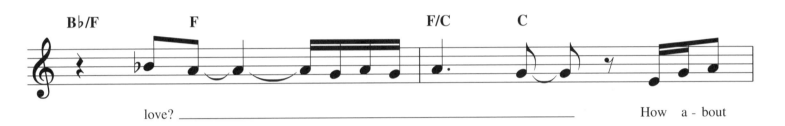

love? ___ How a - bout

love? ___ How a - bout

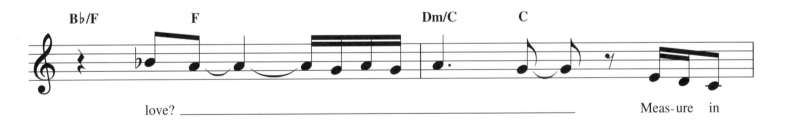

love? ___ Meas-ure in

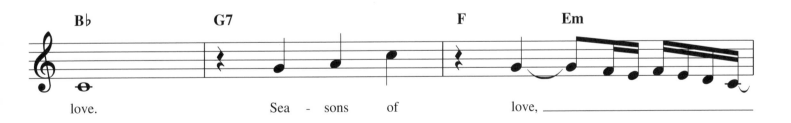

love. Sea - sons of love, ___

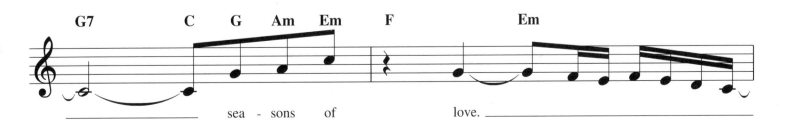

___ sea - sons of love. ___

Five hun - dred twen - ty five thou - sand

six hun - dred min - utes, five hun - dred twen -ty five thou - sand

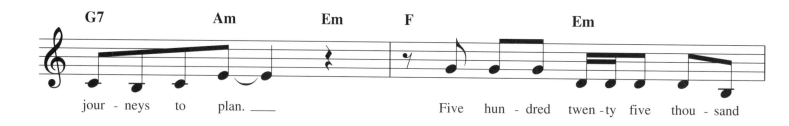

jour - neys to plan. ____ Five hun - dred twen - ty five thou - sand

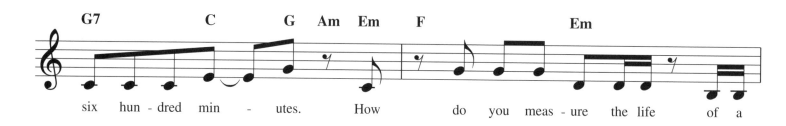

six hun - dred min - utes. How do you meas - ure the life of a

wom - an or ____ a man? ____ In truth that ____ she learned or in

times that ____ he cried, ____ in bridg - es ____ he burned or the

way that she died. _____ It's time now to sing out, though the

sto - ry nev - er ends. _____ Let's cel - e -brate, re -mem - ber a year in the

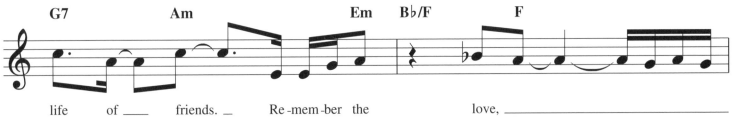

life of ___ friends. _ Re -mem -ber the love, _____

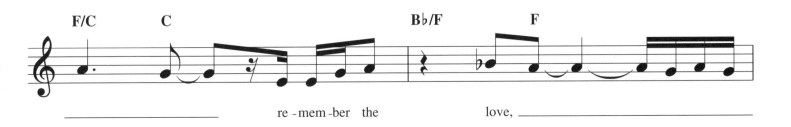

_____ re -mem -ber the love, _____

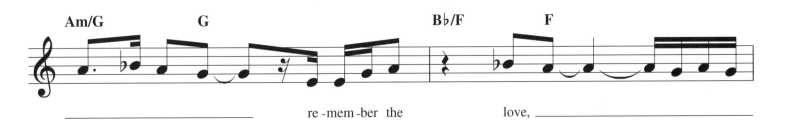

_____ re -mem -ber the love, _____

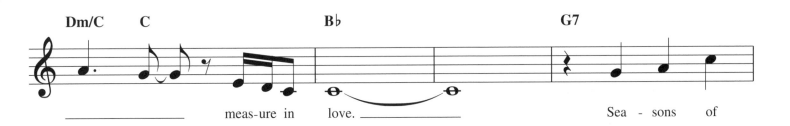

_____ meas -ure in love. _____ Sea - sons of

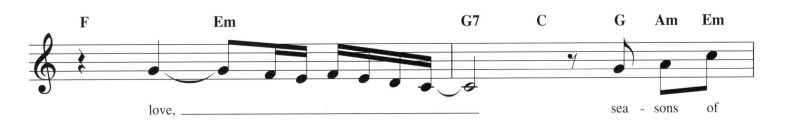

love, _____ sea - sons of

love. _____

SEPTEMBER SONG
from the Musical Play KNICKERBOCKER HOLIDAY

Words by MAXWELL ANDERSON
Music by KURT WEILL

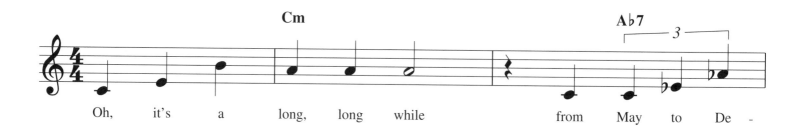

Oh, it's a long, long while from May to De-

cem - ber, _____ but the days grow short,

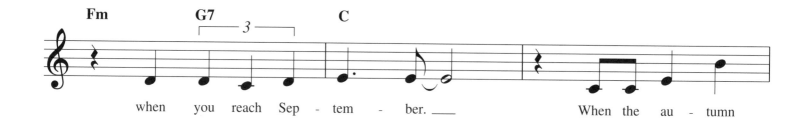

when you reach Sep - tem - ber. _____ When the au - tumn

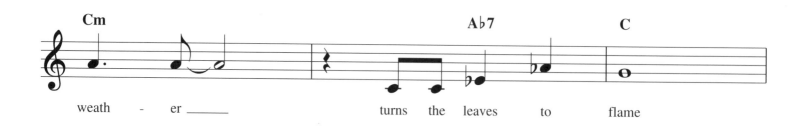

weath - er _____ turns the leaves to flame

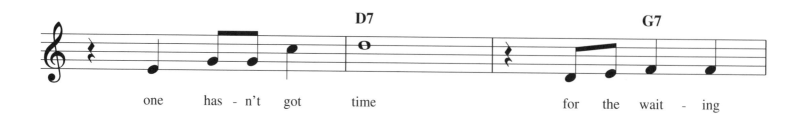

one has - n't got time for the wait - ing

143

game. _____ Oh, the days dwin - dle down _____

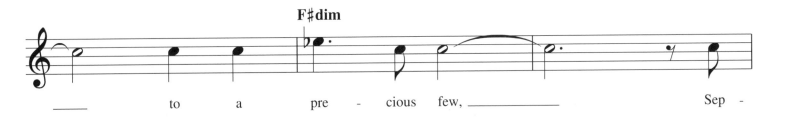

_____ to a pre - cious few, _____ Sep -

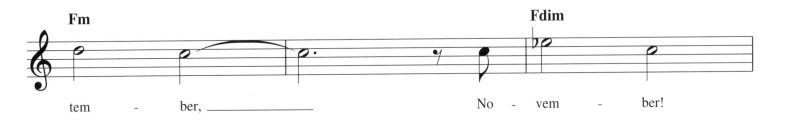

tem - ber, _____ No - vem - ber!

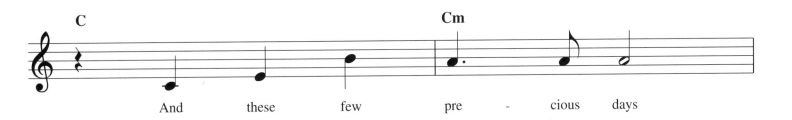

And these few pre - cious days

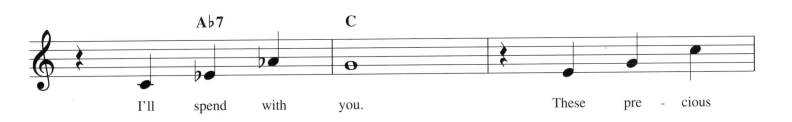

I'll spend with you. These pre - cious

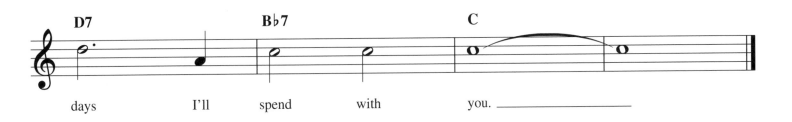

days I'll spend with you. _____

SEVENTY SIX TROMBONES
from Meredith Willson's THE MUSIC MAN

By MEREDITH WILLSON

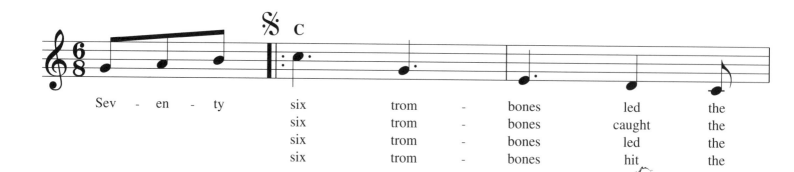

Sev - en - ty six trom - bones led the
six trom - bones caught the
six trom - bones led the
six trom - bones hit the

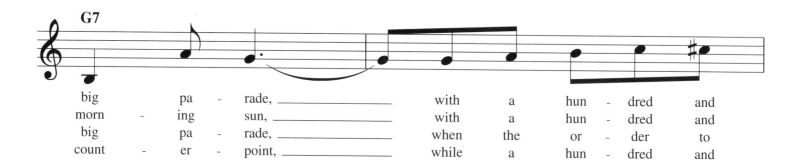

big pa - rade, _____ with a hun - dred and
morn - ing sun, _____ with a hun - dred and
big pa - rade, _____ when the or - der to
count - er - point, _____ while a hun - dred and

ten cor - nets close at hand. They were fol - lowed by
ten cor - nets right be - hind. There were more than a
march rang out loud and clear. Start - ing off with a
ten cor - nets played the air. Then I mod - est - ly

rows and rows of the fin - est vir - tu - o - sos, the
thou - sand reeds spring - ing up like weeds, there were
big bang bong on a Chi - nese gong by a
took my place as the on - ly bass and I

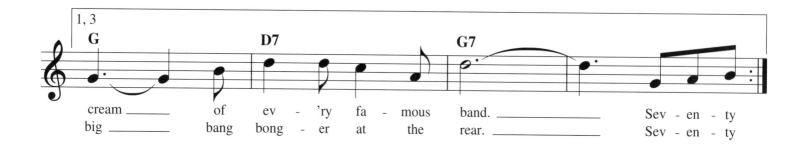

cream _____ of ev - 'ry fa - mous band. _____ Sev - en - ty
big _____ bang bong - er at the rear. _____ Sev - en - ty

SHE (HE) TOUCHED ME

from DRAT! THE CAT!

Lyric by IRA LEVIN
Music by MILTON SCHAFER

SOME ENCHANTED EVENING
from SOUTH PACIFIC

Lyrics by OSCAR HAMMERSTEIN II
Music by RICHARD RODGERS

Some en-chant-ed eve - ning _____ you may see a stran - ger, _____
Some en-chant-ed eve - ning _____ some-one may be laugh - ing, _____

you may see a stran - ger _____ a - cross a crowd - ed room.
you may hear her laugh - ing _____ a - cross a crowd - ed room.

And some-how you know, _____ you know e - ven then _____
And night af - ter night, _____ as strange as it seems _____

_____ that some - where you'll see her a - gain and a -
_____ the sound of her laugh - ter will sing in your

gain. _____
dreams. _____

Who can ex - plain it? Who can tell you why? Fools give you rea - sons,

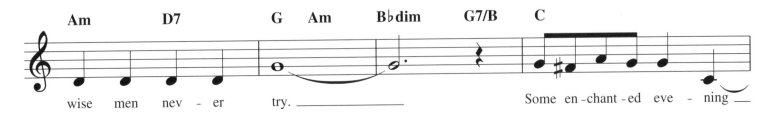

wise men nev - er try. _____ Some en -chant -ed eve - ning _____

_____ when you find your true love, _____

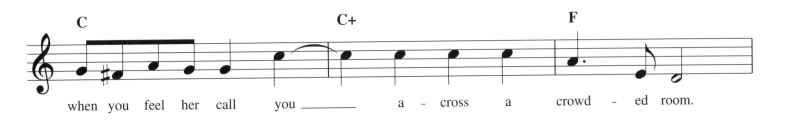

when you feel her call you _____ a - cross a crowd - ed room.

Then fly to her side _____ and make her your own _____

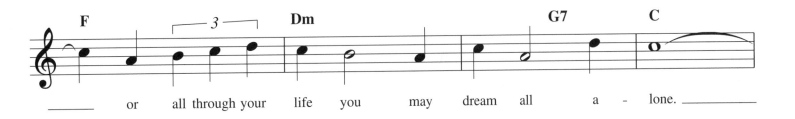

_____ or all through your life you may dream all a - lone. _____

_____ Once you have found her, nev - er let her go.

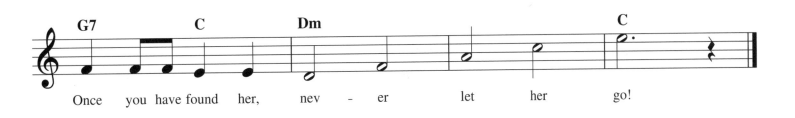

Once you have found her, nev - er let her go!

SOMEONE LIKE YOU

from JEKYLL & HYDE

Words by LESLIE BRICUSSE
Music by FRANK WILDHORN

SOPHISTICATED LADY
from SOPHISTICATED LADIES

Words and Music by DUKE ELLINGTON,
IRVING MILLS and MITCHELL PARISH

They

say _____ in - to your ear - ly life ro - mance came, _____ and in this

heart of yours burned a flame, _____ a flame that flick - ered one day and died a -

way. Then, _____ with dis - il - lu - sion deep in your eyes, _____ you learned that

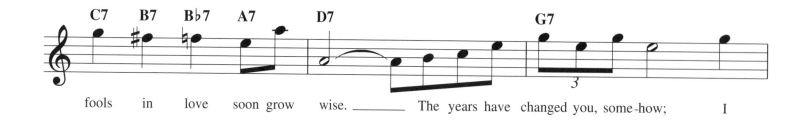

fools in love soon grow wise. _____ The years have changed you, some - how; I

153

see you now...   Smok - ing, drink - ing, nev - er think - ing of to -

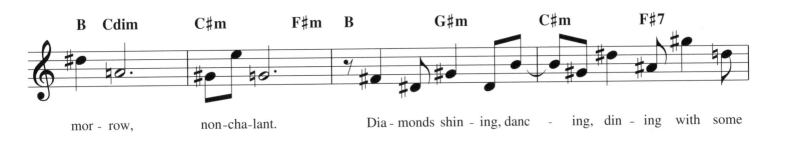

mor - row,   non-cha-lant.   Dia - monds shin - ing, danc - ing, din - ing with some

man   in a res - tau - rant;   is that all you real - ly want?   No, _____ so - phis - ti -

cat - ed la - dy, I   know, _____ you miss the love you lost long a -

go, _____ and when no - bod - y is nigh   you   cry. _____

THE SOUND OF MUSIC
from THE SOUND OF MUSIC

Lyrics by OSCAR HAMMERSTEIN II
Music by RICHARD RODGERS

The hills are a-live with the sound of mu - sic, _____
go to the hills when my heart is lone - ly. _____

_____ with songs they have sung for a thou - sand
_____ I know I will hear what I've heard be -

years. _____ The hills fill my heart with the sound of
fore. _____

mu - sic. _____ My heart wants to sing ev - 'ry

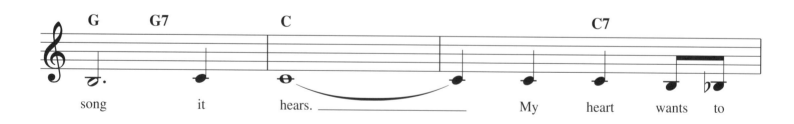

song it hears. _____ My heart wants to

beat like the wings of the birds that rise from the lake to the

trees. My heart wants to sigh like a chime that flies from a

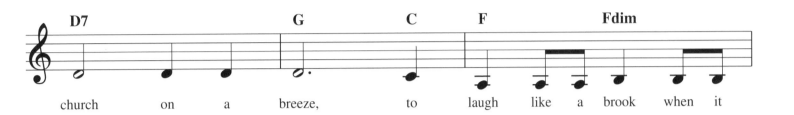

church on a breeze, to laugh like a brook when it

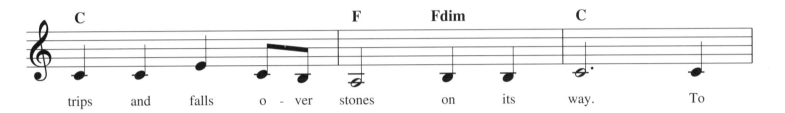

trips and falls o - ver stones on its way. To

D.S. al Coda

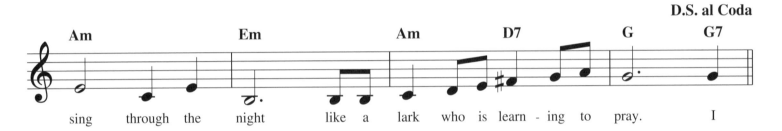

sing through the night like a lark who is learn - ing to pray. I

CODA

____ My heart will be blessed with the sound of

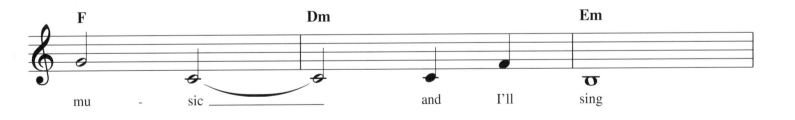

mu - sic _____ and I'll sing

once more. _____

THE SURREY WITH THE FRINGE ON TOP

from OKLAHOMA!

Lyrics by OSCAR HAMMERSTEIN II
Music by RICHARD RODGERS

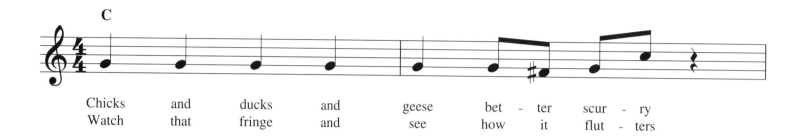

Chicks and ducks and geese bet - ter scur - ry
Watch that fringe and see how it flut - ters

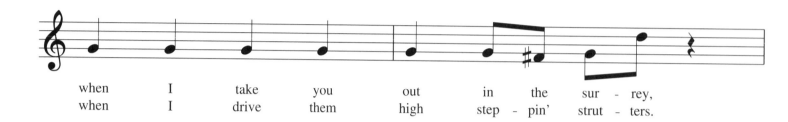

when I take you out in the sur - rey,
when I drive them out high step - pin' strut - ters.

when I take you out in the sur - rey with the
nos - ey pokes 'll peek thru their shut - ters and their

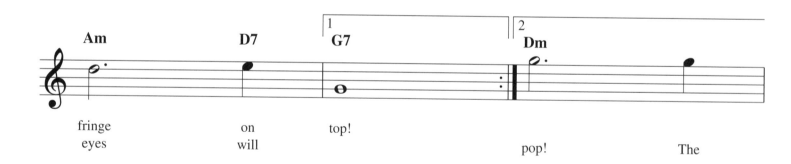

fringe on top!
eyes will pop! The

wheels are yel - ler, the up - hol - ster - y's brown, the

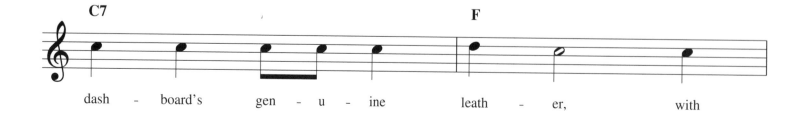

dash - board's gen - u - ine leath - er, with

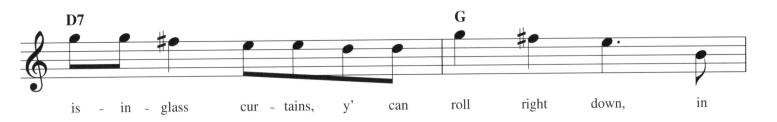

is - in - glass cur - tains, y' can roll right down, in

case there's a change in the weath - er. Two bright side - lights

wink - in' and blink - in', ain't no fin - er

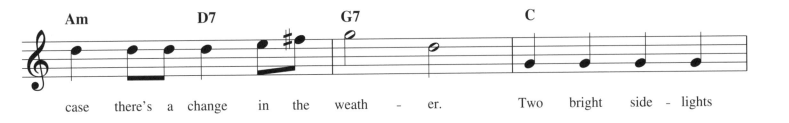

rig I'm a - think - in'. You can keep your

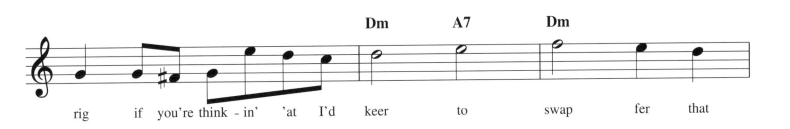

rig if you're think - in' 'at I'd keer to swap fer that

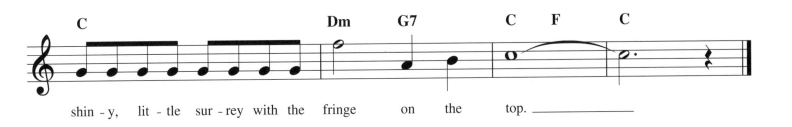

shin - y, lit - tle sur - rey with the fringe on the top. _____

THERE ARE WORSE THINGS I COULD DO

from GREASE

Lyric and Music by WARREN CASEY
and JIM JACOBS

THERE'S A SMALL HOTEL

from ON YOUR TOES

Words by LORENZ HART
Music by RICHARD RODGERS

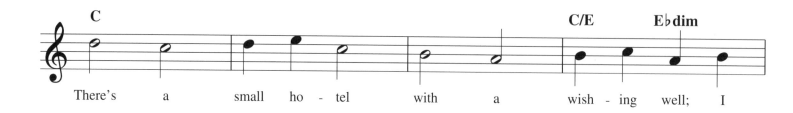

There's a small ho - tel with a wish - ing well; I

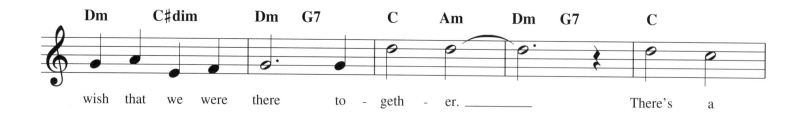

wish that we were there to - geth - er. _____ There's a

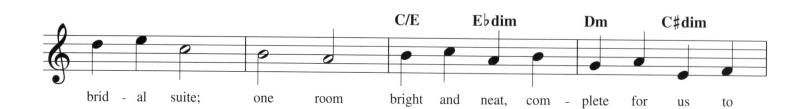

brid - al suite; one room bright and neat, com - plete for us to

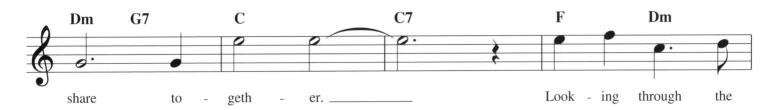

share to - geth - er. _____ Look - ing through the

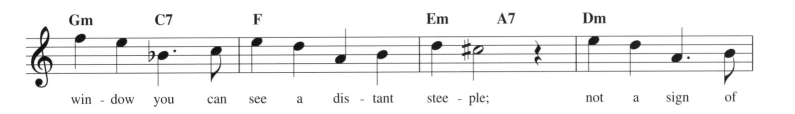

win - dow you can see a dis - tant stee - ple; not a sign of

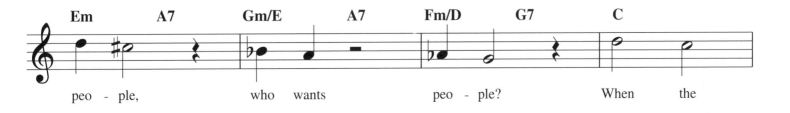

peo - ple, who wants peo - ple? When the

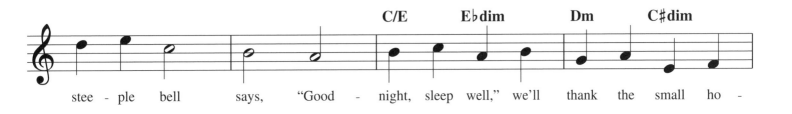

stee - ple bell says, "Good - night, sleep well," we'll thank the small ho -

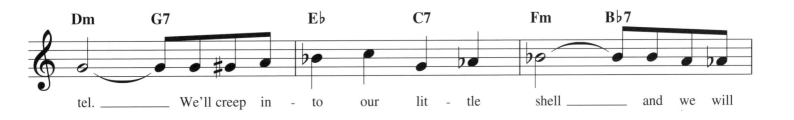

tel. _____ We'll creep in - to our lit - tle shell _____ and we will

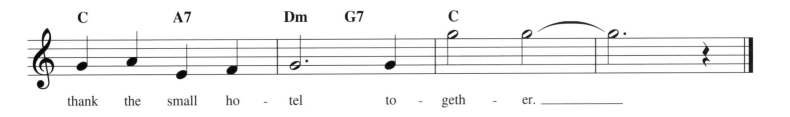

thank the small ho - tel to - geth - er. _____

THERE'S NO BUSINESS LIKE SHOW BUSINESS
from the Stage Production ANNIE GET YOUR GUN

Words and Music by
IRVING BERLIN

163

THEY CALL THE WIND MARIA

from PAINT YOUR WAGON

Words by ALAN JAY LERNER
Music by FREDERICK LOEWE

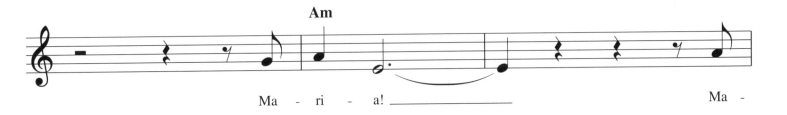

Ma - ri - a! _____ Ma -

ri - a! _____ They call the

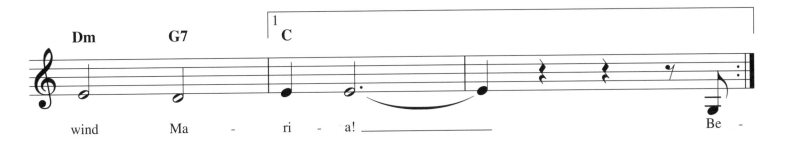

wind Ma - ri - a! _____ Be -

ri - a! _____ Ma - ri - a! _____

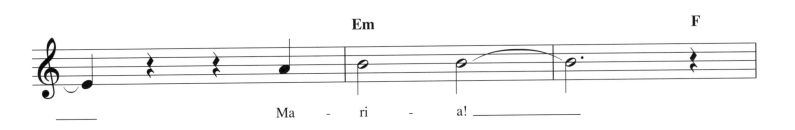

_____ Ma - ri - a! _____

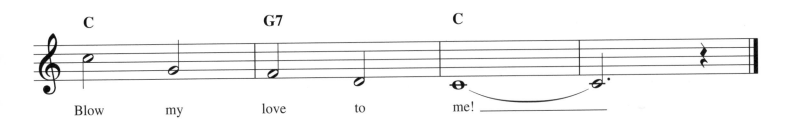

Blow my love to me! _____

THEY SAY IT'S WONDERFUL
from the Stage Production ANNIE GET YOUR GUN

Words and Music by
IRVING BERLIN

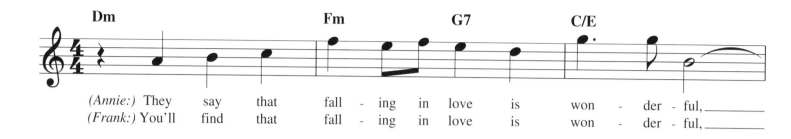

(Annie:) They say that fall - ing in love is won - der - ful,_____
(Frank:) You'll find that fall - ing in love is won - der - ful,_____

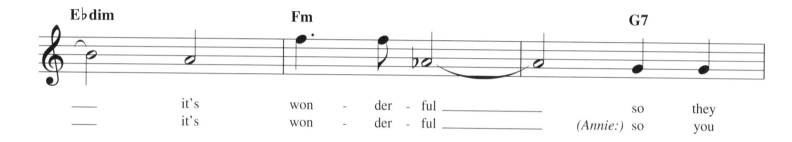

____ it's won - der - ful _____ so they
____ it's won - der - ful _____ (Annie:) so you

say. _____ And with a moon up a - bove, it's
say. _____ (Frank:) And with a moon up a - bove, it's

won - der - ful, _____ it's won - der - ful _____ so they
won - der - ful, _____ it's won - der - ful _____ (Annie:) so you

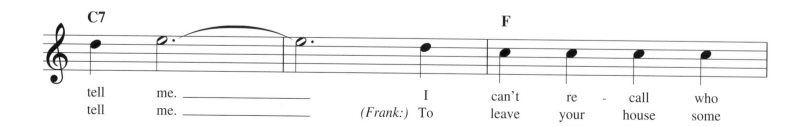

tell me. _____ I can't re - call who
tell me. _____ (Frank:) To leave your house some

said it, I know I nev - er read it, I
morn - ing, and with - out an - y warn - ing, you're

on - ly know they tell me that love is grand, and
stop - ping peo - ple shout - ing that love is grand. And

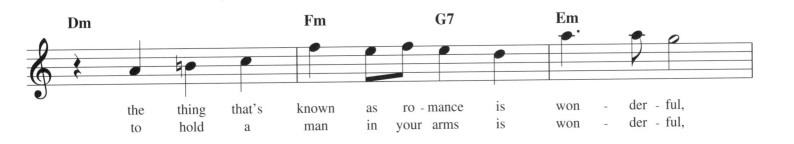

the thing that's known as ro - mance is won - der - ful,
to hold a man in your arms is won - der - ful,

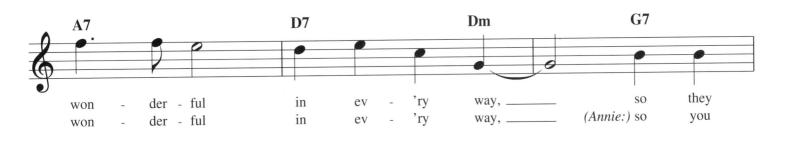

won - der - ful in ev - 'ry way, _____ so they
won - der - ful in ev - 'ry way, _____ *(Annie:)* so you

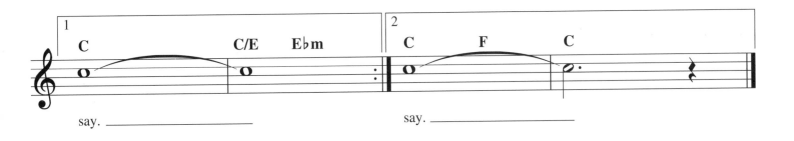

say. _____
say. _____

THOU SWELL
from A CONNECTICUT YANKEE

Words by LORENZ HART
Music by RICHARD RODGERS

TILL THERE WAS YOU
from Meredith Willson's THE MUSIC MAN

By MEREDITH WILLSON

TOGETHER WHEREVER WE GO

from GYPSY

Words by STEPHEN SONDHEIM
Music by JULE STYNE

Wher - ev - er we go, _____ what - ev - er we do, _____

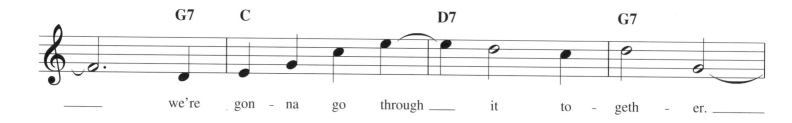

_____ we're gon - na go through _____ it to - geth - er. _____

_____ We may not go far, _____ but sure as a star, _____

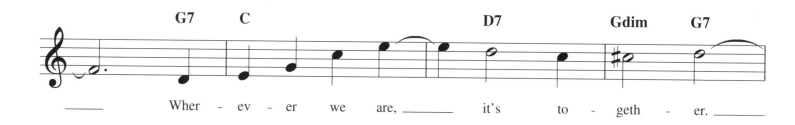

_____ Wher - ev - er we are, _____ it's to - geth - er. _____

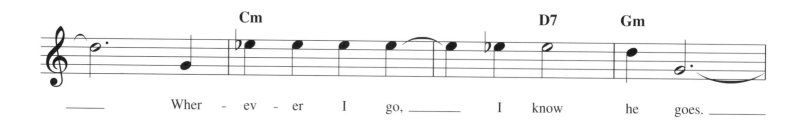

_____ Wher - ev - er I go, _____ I know he goes. _____

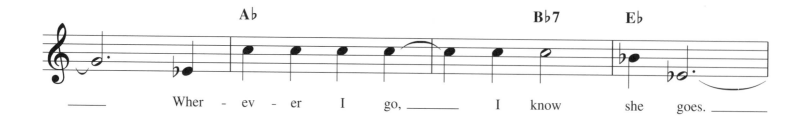

_____ Wher - ev - er I go, _____ I know she goes. _____

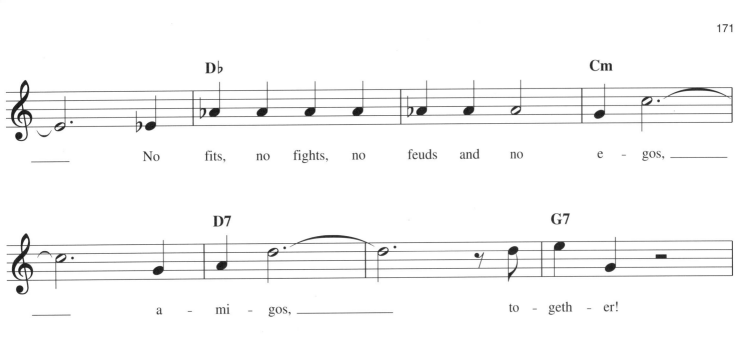

No fits, no fights, no feuds and no e - gos, _____

a - mi - gos, _____ to - geth - er!

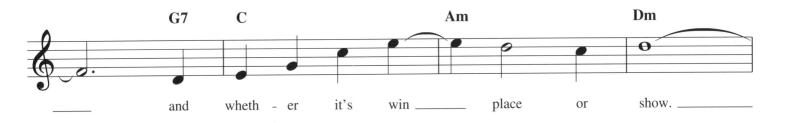

Through thick and through thin, _____ all out or all in, _____

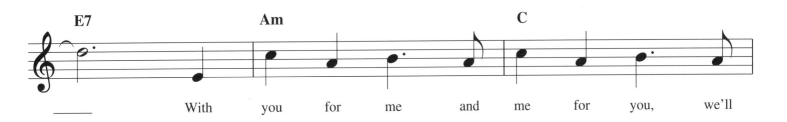

and wheth - er it's win _____ place or show. _____

With you for me and me for you, we'll

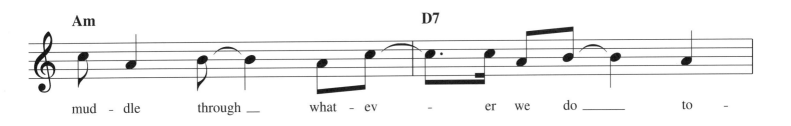

mud - dle through _ what - ev - er we do _____ to -

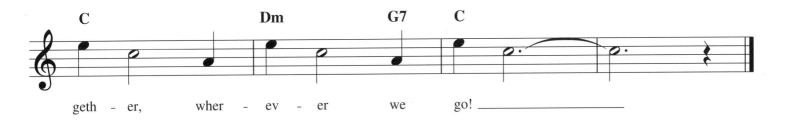

geth - er, wher - ev - er we go! _____

TRY TO REMEMBER
from THE FANTASTICKS

Words by TOM JONES
Music by HARVEY SCHMIDT

UNEXPECTED SONG
from SONG AND DANCE

Music by ANDREW LLOYD WEBBER
Lyrics by DON BLACK

WHAT KIND OF FOOL AM I?

from the Musical Production STOP THE WORLD—I WANT TO GET OFF

Words and Music by LESLIE BRICUSSE
and ANTHONY NEWLEY

WHAT I DID FOR LOVE

from A CHORUS LINE

Music by MARVIN HAMLISCH
Lyric by EDWARD KLEBAN

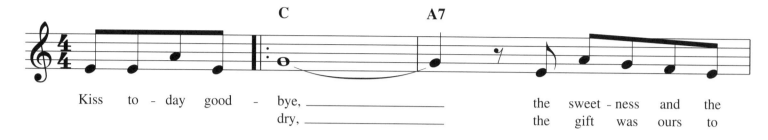

Kiss to - day good - bye, _____ the sweet - ness and the
dry, _____ the gift was ours to

sor - row. _____ We did what we had to
bor - row. _____ It's as if we al - ways

do, _____ and I can't re - gret what I did for love, _
knew, _____ but I won't for - get what I did for love, _

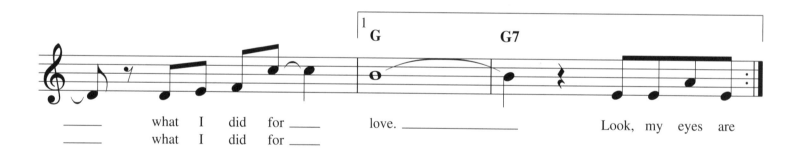

_____ what I did for ____ love. _____ Look, my eyes are
_____ what I did for ____

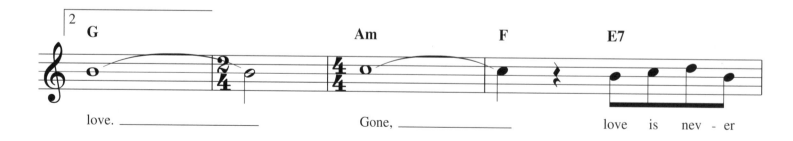

love. _____ Gone, _____ love is nev - er

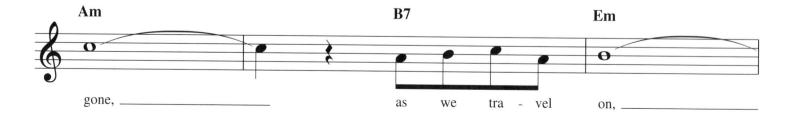

gone, _____ as we tra - vel on, _____

_____ love's what we'll re - mem - ber. Kiss to - day good -

bye, _____ and point me t'ward to - mor - row. _____

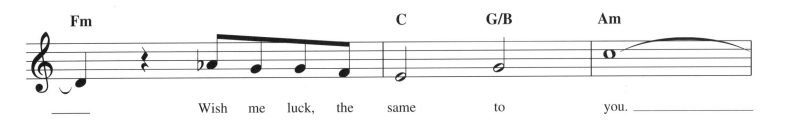

_____ Wish me luck, the same to you. _____

_____ Won't for - get, can't re - gret what I did for

love, what I did for _____ love,

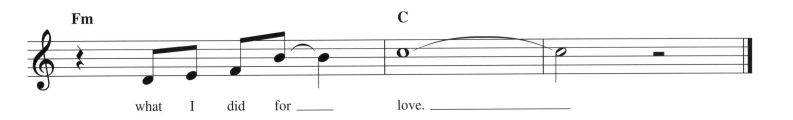

what I did for _____ love. _____

WHERE IS LOVE?

from the Columbia Pictures - Romulus Film OLIVER!

Words and Music by
LIONEL BART

Where _____ is love? Does it fall from skies a-
Where _____ is she who I close my eyes to

bove? Is it un-der-neath the wil-low tree _____ that
see? Will I ev-er know the sweet "Hel-lo," _____ that's

I've been dream-ing of? Who can say where she may
meant for on-ly me? Ev-'ry night I kneel and

hide? Must I tra-vel far _____ and wide?
pray: Let to-mor-row be _____ the day

Till I am be-side the } some-one who I can mean
when I see the face of }

some-thing to where, _____ where _____ is

1 love? _____

2 love? _____

WITH A SONG IN MY HEART

from SPRING IS HERE

Words by LORENZ HART
Music by RICHARD RODGERS

WHERE OR WHEN
from BABES IN ARMS

Words by LORENZ HART
Music by RICHARD RODGERS

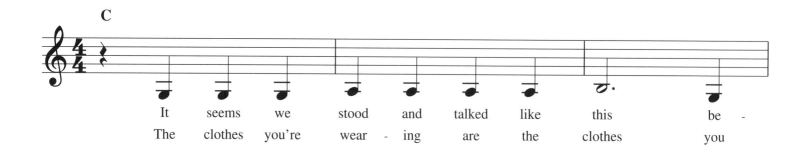

It seems we stood and talked like this be -
The clothes you're wear - ing are the clothes you

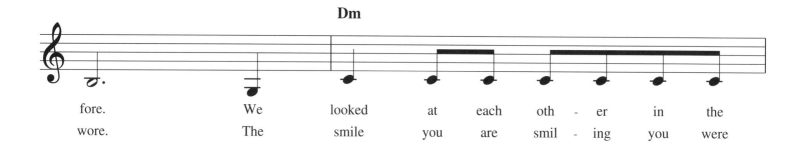

fore.   We looked at each oth - er in the
wore.   The smile you are smil - ing you were

same way then;   but I can't re - mem - ber where or
smil - ing then,   but I can't re - mem - ber where or

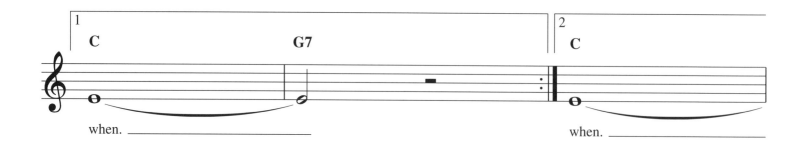

when. _____
when. _____

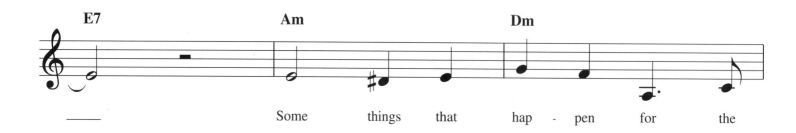

Some things that hap - pen for the

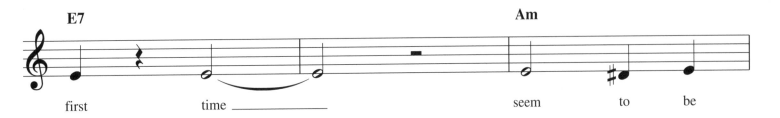

first time _____ seem to be

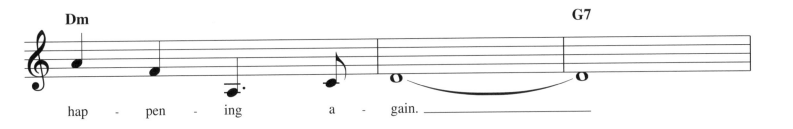

hap - pen - ing a - gain. _____

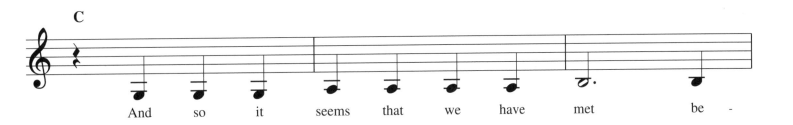

And so it seems that we have met be -

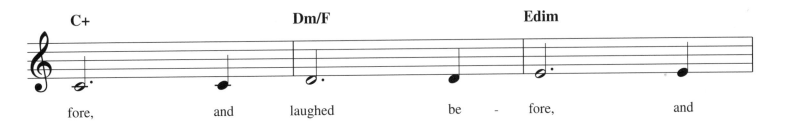

fore, and laughed be - fore, and

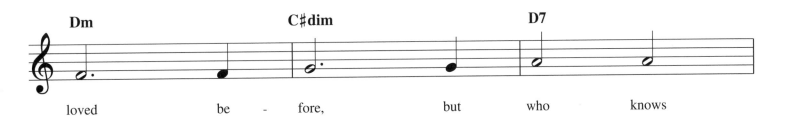

loved be - fore, but who knows

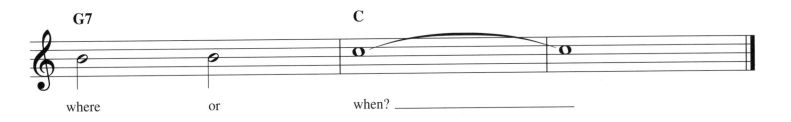

where or when? _____

WHO CAN I TURN TO (WHEN NOBODY NEEDS ME)

from THE ROAR OF THE GREASEPAINT—THE SMELL OF THE CROWD

Words and Music by LESLIE BRICUSSE
and ANTHONY NEWLEY

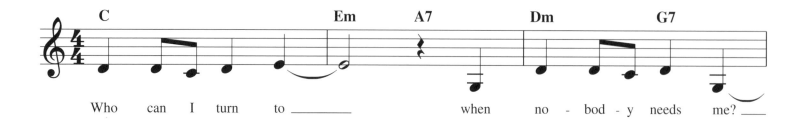

Who can I turn to _____ when no-bod-y needs me? _____

My heart wants to know and so I must go where

des-tin-y leads me. _____ With no star to guide me, _____

_____ and no one be-side me, _____ I'll

go on my way and af-ter the day, the dark-ness will hide me. _____

And may - be to - mor - row _____ I'll

find what I'm af - ter, _____ I'll throw off my sor - row,

beg steal or bor - row my share of laugh - ter. _____ With

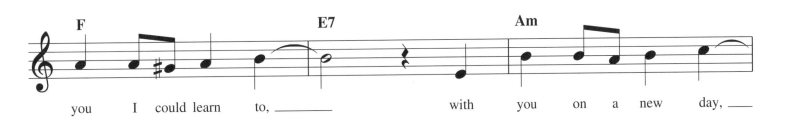

you I could learn to, _____ with you on a new day, ___

___ but who can I turn to if you turn a - way? _____

WOULDN'T IT BE LOVERLY

from MY FAIR LADY

Words by ALAN JAY LERNER
Music by FREDERICK LOEWE

All I want is a room some - where, far a - way from the

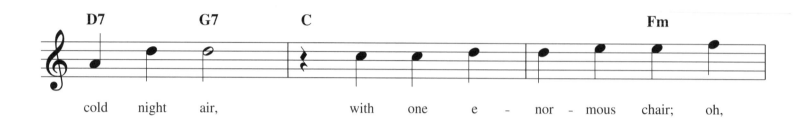

cold night air, with one e - nor - mous chair; oh,

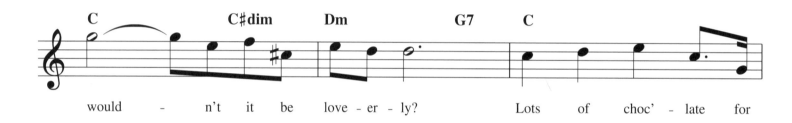

would - n't it be love - er - ly? Lots of choc' - late for

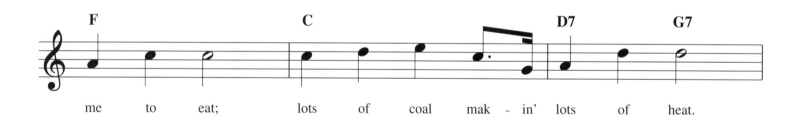

me to eat; lots of coal mak - in' lots of heat.

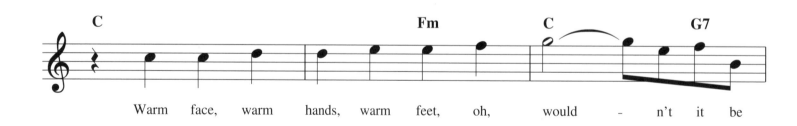

Warm face, warm hands, warm feet, oh, would - n't it be

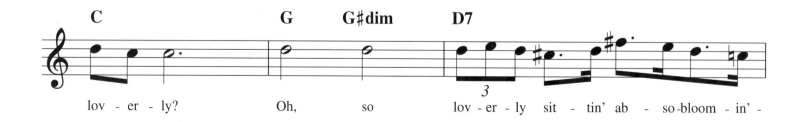

lov - er - ly? Oh, so lov - er - ly sit - tin' ab - so - bloom - in' -

185

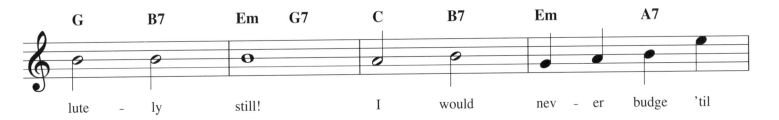

lute - ly   still!   I   would   nev - er budge 'til

spring   crept   o - ver the win - dow sill.   Some - one's   head   rest - in'

on   my   knee;   warm   and   ten - der   as   he   can   be;

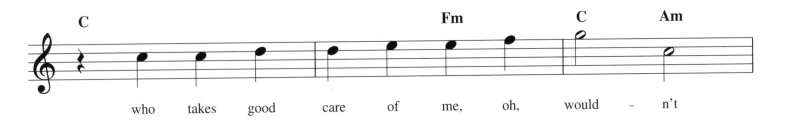

who   takes   good   care   of   me,   oh,   would - n't

it   be   lov - er - ly?   Lov - er - ly!

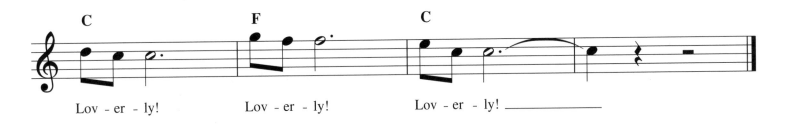

Lov - er - ly!   Lov - er - ly!   Lov - er - ly! _____

YOU'LL NEVER WALK ALONE
from CAROUSEL

Lyrics by OSCAR HAMMERSTEIN II
Music by RICHARD RODGERS

When you walk through a storm hold your head up

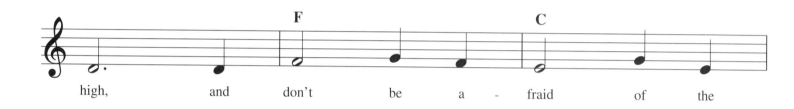

high, and don't be a - fraid of the

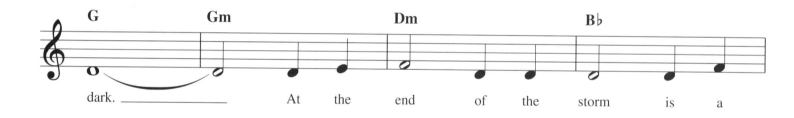

dark. _____ At the end of the storm is a

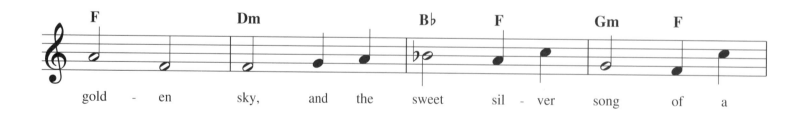

gold - en sky, and the sweet sil - ver song of a

lark. _____ Walk on through the wind, walk

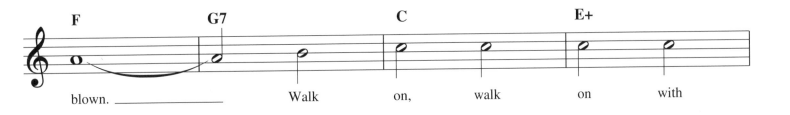

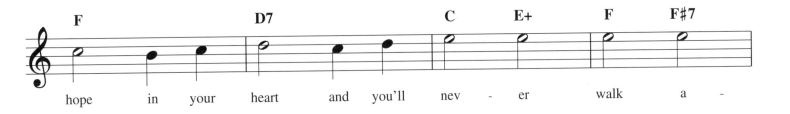

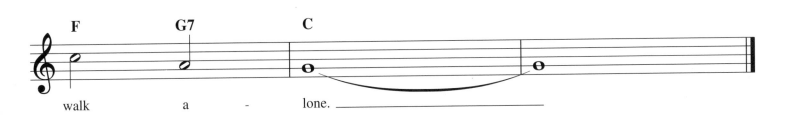

YOUNGER THAN SPRINGTIME
from SOUTH PACIFIC

Lyrics by OSCAR HAMMERSTEIN II
Music by RICHARD RODGERS

Young - er than spring - time are you, Soft - er than star - light

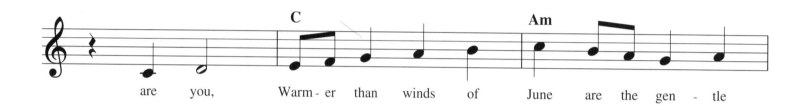

are you, Warm - er than winds of June are the gen - tle

lips you gave me. Gay - er than laugh - ter are you,

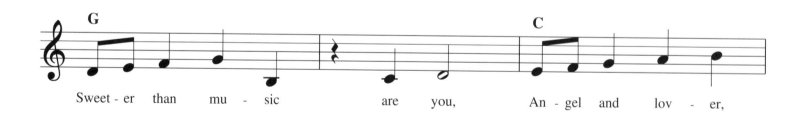

Sweet - er than mu - sic are you, An - gel and lov - er,

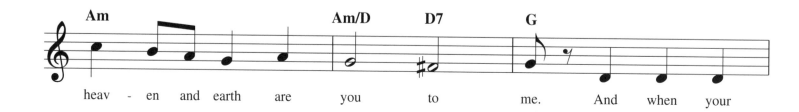

heav - en and earth are you to me. And when your

youth and joy in - vade my arms And fill my

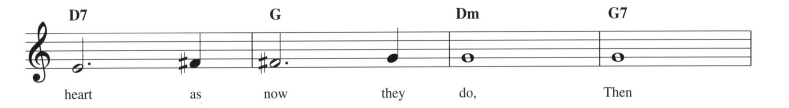

heart as now they do, Then

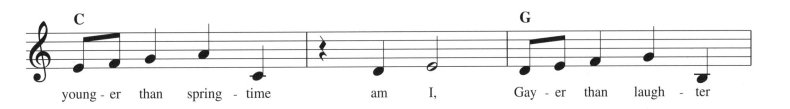

young - er than spring - time am I, Gay - er than laugh - ter

am I, An - gel and lov - er, heav - en and earth am

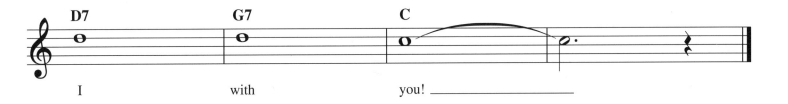

I with you! _____

CHORD SPELLER

C chords

C	C–E–G
Cm	C–E♭–G
C7	C–E–G–B♭
Cdim	C–E♭–G♭
C+	C–E–G♯

C♯ or D♭ chords

C♯	C♯–F–G♯
C♯m	C♯–E–G♯
C♯7	C♯–F–G♯–B
C♯dim	C♯–E–G
C♯+	C♯–F–A

D chords

D	D–F♯–A
Dm	D–F–A
D7	D–F♯–A–C
Ddim	D–F–A♭
D+	D–F♯–A♯

E♭ chords

E♭	E♭–G–B♭
E♭m	E♭–G♭–B♭
E♭7	E♭–G–B♭–D♭
E♭dim	E♭–G♭–A
E♭+	E♭–G–B

E chords

E	E–G♯–B
Em	E–G–B
E7	E–G♯–B–D
Edim	E–G–B♭
E+	E–G♯–C

F chords

F	F–A–C
Fm	F–A♭–C
F7	F–A–C–E♭
Fdim	F–A♭–B
F+	F–A–C♯

F♯ or G♭ chords

F♯	F♯–A♯–C♯
F♯m	F♯–A–C♯
F♯7	F♯–A♯–C♯–E
F♯dim	F♯–A–C
F♯+	F♯–A♯–D

G chords

G	G–B–D
Gm	G–B♭–D
G7	G–B–D–F
Gdim	G–B♭–D♭
G+	G–B–D♯

G♯ or A♭ chords

A♭	A♭–C–E♭
A♭m	A♭–B–E♭
A♭7	A♭–C–E♭–G♭
A♭dim	A♭–B–D
A♭+	A♭–C–E

A chords

A	A–C♯–E
Am	A–C–E
A7	A–C♯–E–G
Adim	A–C–E♭
A+	A–C♯–F

B♭ chords

B♭	B♭–D–F
B♭m	B♭–D♭–F
B♭7	B♭–D–F–A♭
B♭dim	B♭–D♭–E
B♭+	B♭–D–F♯

B chords

B	B–D♯–F♯
Bm	B–D–F♯
B7	B–D♯–F♯–A
Bdim	B–D–F
B+	B–D♯–G

Important Note: A slash chord (C/E, G/B) tells you that a certain bass note is to be played under a particular harmony. In the case of C/E, the chord is C and the bass note is E.

HAL LEONARD PRESENTS
FAKE BOOKS FOR BEGINNERS!

THE EASY FAKE BOOK

This follow-up to the popular *Your First Fake Book* features over 100 more songs for even beginning-level musicians to enjoy. This volume features the same larger notation with simplified harmonies and melodies with all songs in the key of C. In addition, this edition features introductions for each song, adding a more finished sound to the arrangements! Songs include: Alfie • All I Ask of You • Always on My Mind • Angel • Autumn in New York • Blue Skies • Fields of Gold • Grow Old With Me • Hey, Good Lookin' • I'll Be There • Imagine • Memory • Misty • My Heart Will Go on (Love Theme from 'Titanic') • People • Stand by Me • Star Dust • Tears in Heaven • Unchained Melody • What a Wonderful World • and more.

_____00240144 ....$19.95

THE SIMPLIFIED FAKE BOOK

The sequel to *Your First Fake Book* and *The Easy Fake Book*, this new collection includes 100 favorite songs all in the key of C, complete with lyrics and simplified chords that remain true to the tune. It also features easy-to-read, large music notation that beginning or older players will love. The songs come from all musical genres: standards, rock 'n' roll, Broadway and the movies, and more! Songs include: Bad, Bad Leroy Brown • Besame Mucho (Kiss Me Much) • Change the World • Could I Have This Dance • Endless Love • Fever • Fire and Rain • From a Distance • I've Grown Accustomed to Her Face • It's a Small World • Piano Man • The Rainbow Connection • Sentimental Journey • Sunshine on My Shoulders • That's Amore (That's Love) • There's No Business like Show Business • Twist and Shout • Unexpected Song • Yellow Submarine • You Are My Sunshine • You'll Be in My Heart (Pop Version) • and more.

_____00240168 ....$19.95

THE EASY GOSPEL FAKE BOOK

A beginning fake book for players new to "faking"! This great collection contains over 100 favorite Gospel songs all in the key of C. Each song features lyrics and simplified chords that remain true to each original tune, with large, easy-to-read music notation. Includes: Amazing Grace • At Calvary • Because He Lives • Blessed Assurance • Church in the Wildwood • Do Lord • Give Me That Old Time Religion • He Touched Me • Higher Ground • His Eye Is on the Sparrow • His Name Is Wonderful • How Great Thou Art • I Bowed on My Knees and Cried Holy • I Saw the Light • I'll Fly Away • In the Garden • Just a Closer Walk with Thee • Mansion over the Hilltop • More Than Wonderful • The Old Rugged Cross • Precious Lord, Take My Hand • Precious Memories • Put Your Hand in the Hand • Rock of Ages • Shall We Gather at the River? • Sweet By and By • Turn Your Radio On • Upon This Rock • When the Roll Is Called Up Yonder • Whispering Hope • Will the Circle Be Unbroken • Wings of a Dove • and dozens more!

_____00240169 ....$19.95

THE EASY BROADWAY FAKE BOOK

Another book in this popular series featuring over 100 great Broadway tunes, all in the key of C with large, easy-to-read notation. Songs include: All I Ask of You • Any Dream Will Do • Beauty and the Beast • Bring Him Home • Comedy Tonight • Edelweiss • Getting to Know You • I've Grown Accustomed to Her Face • The Impossible Dream (The Quest) • Let Me Entertain You • Luck Be a Lady • Memory • The Music of the Night • One • People • Seasons of Love • September Song • What I Did for Love • and more.

_____00240180 ....$19.95

YOUR FIRST FAKE BOOK

An entry-level fake book! This book features larger-than-most fake book notation with simplified harmonies and melodies – and all songs are in the key of C. An introduction addresses basic instruction in playing from a fake book. Includes over 100 songs, including: Ain't Misbehavin' • All the Things You Are • America the Beautiful • Beauty and the Beast • Bewitched • Blueberry Hill • Can't Help Falling in Love • Don't Get Around Much Anymore • Edelweiss • Getting to Know You • Heart and Soul • It Only Takes a Moment • Leaving on a Jet Plane • Let It Be • Love Me Tender • Maria • Mood Indigo • Satin Doll • Somewhere Out There • Try to Remember • When the Saints Go Marching In • Young at Heart • more.

_____00240112 ....$19.95

Prices, contents and availability subject to change without notice.

For More Information, See Your Local Music Dealer,
or Write To:

HAL•LEONARD® CORPORATION
7777 W. Bluemound Rd. P.O. Box 13819 Milwaukee, WI 53213

www.halleonard.com